The Wonder of It All

Mystery and Meaning in Scripture

Morris Inch

University Press of America,® Inc.
Lanham · Boulder · New York · Toronto · Plymouth, UK

Copyright © 2009 by
University Press of America,® Inc.
4501 Forbes Boulevard
Suite 200
Lanham, Maryland 20706
UPA Acquisitions Department (301) 459-3366

Estover Road
Plymouth PL6 7PY
United Kingdom

Library of Congress Control Number: 2009933218
ISBN-13: 978-0-7618-4802-8 (paperback : alk. paper)
ISBN-10: 0-7618-4802-9 (paperback : alk. paper)
eISBN-13: 978-0-7618-4812-7
eISBN-10: 0-7618-4812-6

CONTENTS

Contents

PREFACE

C. S. Lewis made the apt observation that error generally appears as pairs of opposites. So it is that when we attempt to escape a problem on the one hand, we are likely to fall prey to the opposite. As a prime example, we either minimize the persisting mystery or apparent meaning of Scripture. With such in mind, the present text is an attempt to cultivate a needed balance.

Mystery first invites our attention. Paul observes, "we speak of God's secret wisdom, a wisdom that has been hidden and that God destined for our glory before time began" (1 Cor. 2:7). In the singular, "the term 'mystery' ordinarily refers to something formerly hidden in God and from *all* human eyes but now revealed in history through Christ and made understandable to his people through the Spirit."[1]

Even so, it is *understandable* only in a qualified sense. "For we know in part and we prophesy in part, but when perfection comes, the imperfect disappears" (1 Cor. 13:9). In a manner of speaking, we view matters from the middle—with reference to paradise lost and regained.

Mystery is primarily associated with God and his initiatives. The nearest analogy concerns other individuals. Qualifications aside, we get to know a person only insofar as he or she will allow.

The notion of mystery also extends to creation. First in one connection, and then another—with little exception. All this has to do with what Peter Berger graphically describes as a *Sacred Canopy*. As for commentary, "Seen in the perspective of society, every nomos is an area of meaning carved out of a vast mass of meaninglessness, a small clearing of lucidity in a formless, dark, always ominous jungle."[2] In this manner, order supplants chaos.

Accordingly, the Lord declares: "Heaven is my throne, and the earth is my footstool" (Isa. 66:11). "This means that God can be worshiped equally as Transcendent Being and as Immanent Friend. Because of this there is no need for a special 'house' where God is to be bound, for 'the place of rest' cannot be confined to a building made by human hands."[3]

We turn our attention from *mystery* to *meaning*, with a common sense approach to interpreting Scripture. Initially, by way of exploring the implications of divine significance of context, an introduction to general hermeneutics, and ethical implications.

Then, by way of illustration, with two case studies. First, concerning Genesis as an account for why life appears as we find it. Second, as touches on Luke/Acts—combining an account of the life and ministry of Jesus with that of the early church. All things considered, we engage the mystery and meaning of Scripture in a creative tension.

Morris A. Inch
Russellville, Arkansas
May, 2009

ACKNOWLEDGMENT

While it may seem redundant, I am genuinely appreciative of my wife Joan's gracious assistance in editing and formatting yet another text for publication.

PART ONE

PART ONE

1

ULTIMATE MYSTERY

The ultimate mystery concerns our encounter with the sovereign ruler of the universe. This incites in us a sense of *awe*, which consists of a mixture of reverence, dread, and wonder. As for commentary, "the known must be balanced by the unknown, that God is a *mysterium tremendum et fascinans*, compelling the worshiper with awe toward him but remaining ultimately beyond the grasp of human reason and imagination."[1]

C. S. Lewis proposes a simple exercise. Suppose you heard a tiger growling at the door, and scratching at its panels. You would feel threatened, and hope it would not succeed in gaining entry.

Now, were it a ghost, no natural barrier could refuse its entrance. Were it akin to Casper—the friendly ghost, there would be nothing to fear. Still, one would be unnerved and intimidated by an alien visitor.

Finally, imagine being pursued by Francis Thompson's resolute *Hound of Heaven*.

> I fled Him, down the nights and down the days;
> I fled Him, down the arches of the years;
> I fled Him, down the labyrinthine ways
> Of my own mind; and in the mist of tears.

It is all to no avail, since there is no place to hide from his relentless pursuit.

Two prime examples will suffice to illustrate what is involved. First, Moses was tending the flock of his father-in-law Jethro, and approached Horeb (Sinai)—the mountain of God. It was designated *the mountain of God* either because of past associations, later circumstances, or some combination of the two. In any case, the angel of the Lord appeared to him in a flaming bush that was not consumed.

"Natural explanations for the burning bush have been plentiful, from bushes that exude flammable gas to those covered with brightly colored leaves or berries."[2] Otherwise, one simply opts for something more out of the ordinary.

So Moses reflected, "I will go over and see this strange sight—why the bush does not burn up" (Exod. 3:3).

Whereupon, God called out to him: "Moses! Moses!"

Moses replied in compliant manner, "Here I am."

"Do not come any closer," God cautioned him. "Take off your sandals, for the place where you are standing is holy ground." There are two possible origins for the removal of one's sandals as a mark of reverence. "First, it may be the sign of acceptance of a servant's position, for a slave usually went barefoot. Secondly, it may be a relic of very early days when men laid aside all covering and pretense to approach their God."[3] In any case, one was to draw near only when invited to do so.

The voice continued: "I am the God of your father, the God of Abraham, the God of Isaac and the God of Jacob." This, in turn, recalls the patriarchal narratives, and the manner in which God worked in the past. Moreover, it serves to confirm the validity of his promises.

"At this, Moses hid his face, because he was afraid to look at God." In the presence of a Holy God, the irresistible feeling of our unworthiness is overwhelming.

"I have indeed seen the misery of my people in Egypt," the Almighty informs him, "and I am concerned about their suffering." An encounter with God normally has wider implications than for simply the person involved.

"So I have come down to rescue them from the hand of the Egyptians and to bring them up out of that land into a good and spacious land, a land flowing with milk and honey." The dire straights of the Israelites was chronicled earlier. It seems that they had greatly multiplied, and were perceived as a threat to the Egyptian dynasty. "Come," the ruler urged his retinue, "we must deal shrewdly with them or they will become even more numerous and, if war breaks out, will join our enemies, fight against us and leave the country" (Exod. 1:10). So they put taskmasters over them, and oppressed them with forced labor. Not content with these harsh measures, the king ordered that all Hebrew male children be eliminated. This amounted to genocide.

A land flowing with milk and honey provides an idyllic portrait from a pastoral perspective. In other words, it was rich in natural resources, and quite capable of supporting a displaced people.

"And now the cry of the Israelites has reached me, and I have seen the way the Egyptians are oppressing them. So now, go. I am sending you to Pharaoh to bring my people the Israelites out of Egypt" (3:9). Accordingly, we are to anticipate their deliverance from bondage.

"Who am I that I should go to Pharaoh and bring the Israelites out of Egypt?" Moses understandably protested. "Self-distrust is good, but only if it leads to trust in God. Otherwise it ends as spiritual paralysis, inability and unwillingness to undertake any course of action."[4]

Whereupon, God said: "I will be with you. And this will be the sign to you that it is I who have sent you. When you have brought the people out of Egypt, you will worship God on this mountain." *I will be with you* serves as a pledge that Moses will lack nothing necessary to fulfill his mission. The subsequent worship of God at this location would demonstrate that the Almighty was indeed with him, and had commissioned him for service.

"Suppose I go to the Israelites and say to them, 'The God of your fathers has sent me to you,'" Moses speculated, "and they ask me, 'What is his name?' Then what shall I tell them?" This was equivalent to asking what new revelation Moses had received.

God replied, "I AM who I AM. This is what you shall say to the Israelites, 'I AM has sent me to you.'" God simply *is*, in contrast to the proliferation of lifeless pagan idols. As such, he will make his ways known in subsequent events. In this manner, the sense of mystery is retained.

God also instructed Moses: "Say to the Israelites, 'The LORD (YHWH), the God of your fathers . . . has sent me to you.' This is my name forever, the name by which I am to be remembered from generation to generation." The pious Jews of later times were reluctant to employ the name *Yahweh* lest they risk taking his name in vain. With the passing of time it came to stand for what the name Jesus communicates to Christians as evidence of God's grace.

The narrative reaches its climax at this juncture. It remained for God to work out his intent, overriding the reluctance of his prophet, engaging the Egyptian pantheon, delivering his oppressed people, and covenanting with them at Sinai. Afterward, he would sustain them in the wilderness, enable them for the conquest, guide them through the turbulent time of the Judges, and fine-tuning the monarchy to its covenant obligations. Still later, in sustaining them during the critical time of the exile, and restoring a remnant to the promised land. All things considered, in anticipation of the Messianic Age—as fulfillment of God's righteous agenda.

The scene shifts. "In the year that King Uzziah died, I saw the Lord seated on a throne, high and exalted, and the train of his robe filled the temple" (Isa. 6:1). "Isaiah had witnessed the rapid development of Judah into a strong commercial and military state. Under Uzziah, Judah had attained a degree of strength and prosperity which she had not enjoyed since the days of Solomon."[5] While pride contributed to his downfall, his demise brought to an end an era indicative of God's blessing.

Isaiah commanded an honored place among the prophets. "What manner of man is the prophet?" Abraham Heschel rhetorically inquires. "To us a single act of injustice—cheating in business, exploitation of the poor—is slight; to the prophets, a disaster. To us injustice is injurious to the welfare of the people; to the prophets it is a deathblow to existence; to us, an episode; to them, a catastrophe."[6] In brief, it was their unenviable task to act as a conscience for corporate society.

God is revealed in his regal splendor. In this manner, we are reminded that while many persons are implicated in the course of time, the Almighty remains constant. Consequently, salvation history can be described as *the acts of God.*

"Above him were seraphs, each with six wings. With two wings they covered their faces, with two they covered their feet, and with two they were flying. And they were calling to one another: 'Holy, holy, holy is the Lord Almighty; the whole earth is full of his glory.'" The seraphim were an angelic order. In this regard, they showed deference and rendered service.

Holy thrice repeated is the Lord Almighty. The term *holy* is derived from the notion of separation from all that is insidious, and consecration to what is pure. As such, it constitutes the chief attribute of God. It, moreover, is meant to characterize those who would serve him. In this connection, "Consecrate yourselves and be holy, because I am the Lord your God" (Lev. 20:7).

Conversely, God's *glory* pertains to his regal splendor. It is said to permeate all the earth. "Be exalted, O God, above the heavens;" the psalmist earnestly petitions, "let your glory be over all the earth" (57:5, 11).

At the sound of the seraphs' voices, "the doorposts and thresholds shook and the temple was filled with smoke." This, in turn, is reminiscent of God's manifestation at Sinai. On that occasion, there was lightning and thunder and the "smoke billowed up from it like smoke from a furnace, the whole mountain trembled violently" (Exod. 19:18)—as if associated with volcanic activity.

"Woe to me!" Isaiah cries aloud. "I am ruined. For I am a man of unclean lips, and I live among a people of unclean lips, and my eyes have seen the King, the Lord Almighty." In this manner, the contrast is made between a holy God and a deviant people. Not only is Isaiah personally at fault, but he bears the reproach of accommodating to those around him.

While not entirely unaware of the situation, it is brought home to him by his encounter with the Almighty. As noted earlier, one feels intensely his or her unworthiness. Conversely, there remains no consolation in comparing oneself to others, either in general or concerning some particular. Such as the person who while admitting his proclivity, professes a lack of hypocrisy.

"Then one of the seraphs flew to me with a live coal in his hand, which he had taken with tongs from the altar. With it he touched my mouth and said, 'See, this has touched your lips; your guilt is taken away and your sin is atoned for.'" The imagery is perhaps derived from the altar of incense, thus signifying that his implied petition is favorably received. In any case, he is cleansed.

Whereupon, the prophet hears the voice of the Lord saying: "Whom shall I send? And who will go for us?" The shift from singular to plural is likely an instance of the royal prerogative, as when the potentate says: "It seems good to *us*," rather than to *me*.

"Here I am," Isaiah volunteers. "Send me!" While his zeal is praiseworthy, he is unaware of the cost implicated.

"Go," God replies, "and tell this people: 'Be ever hearing, but never understanding; be ever seeing, but never perceiving.' Make the hearing of this people callous; make their ears dull and close their eyes." So as to confirm them in their intransigence.

"For how long, O Lord" the prophet inquires. It no doubt seems unlikely to him that the Lord will continue to reject his people. The psalmist confidently reflects, "The Lord is compassionate and gracious, slow to anger, abounding in love. He will not always accuse, nor will he harbor his anger forever" (103:8-9).

Then the Lord answered, "Until the cities lie ruined and without inhabitants . . . so the holy seed will be the stump in the land." Only a stump (remnant) will survive, to enjoy restoration. It serves as a stark portrait reflecting the critical insight of the prophet. "The prophet is human, yet he employs notes one octave too high for our ears. He experiences moments that defy our understanding. Often his words begin to burn where conscience ends."[7]

In retrospect, I have chosen extraordinary examples of our encounter with the Almighty, so as to exaggerate the point. Whereas our experience of the transcendent deity is more often of a much milder sort. David Myers elaborates with his provocative discussion of *the mystery of the ordinary*. "Looking for mystery in things bizarre, we feel cheated when later we learn that a hoax or a simple process explains it away," he allows. "All the while we miss the awesome events occurring before, or even within, our very eyes. The extraordinary within the ordinary."[8]

Myers cites the remarkable way in which we encode incoming information. In greater detail, "Our brains operate rather like General Motors, with a few important matters decided by the chair of the board, and everything else, thankfully, handled automatically, effortlessly, and usually competently by amazing intricate mechanisms."[9]

I find fortuitous timing a further helpful illustration. Such as when someone unexpectedly shows up just when his or her input was needed. Or when circumstances fall into place to achieve some worthwhile purpose.

This is by way of refuting the common impression of *the god of the gaps*. That is to say, to overlook the extraordinary in the ordinary. As a result, we limit the sphere of God's activity to events seemingly incapable of being explained on natural grounds. Then, with increased understanding, to shrink his domain yet more. Conversely, Myers seems intent on saying that while God is explicit in nothing, he is implicit in everything.

Persons who exhibit an ongoing awareness of God's presence find it exceedingly reassuring. It is as if they sense being cared for by a compassionate parent, and greatly beloved. All of which brings us full circle, back to Berger's notion of a sacred canopy. Thereby we are encouraged by God's Word, sustained by his grace, and comforted in our affliction.

2

PARADOXICAL MYSTERY

A *paradox* is a statement that at face value seems contradictory. For instance, in conclusion to John Donne's sonnet *Death Be not Proud*: "Death, thou shall die." In this instance, the confession of God as three in one.

C. S. Lewis sets out to dispel the notion that the topic of the Trinity concerns only the theologically elite. An ordinary Christian kneels down to say his prayers. He is trying to get in touch with the Almighty. "He knows that what is prompting him to pray is also God; God, so to speak, inside him. But he also knows that all his real knowledge of God comes through Christ (who) is standing beside him, helping him to pray, praying for him."[1]

"People already knew about God in a vague way," Lewis continues. "Then came a man who claimed to be God; and yet He was not the sort of man you could dismiss as a lunatic." They came to believe in him. Afterward, he was put to death. Death, however, could not restrain him. In due time, his disciples were bonded together into a fellowship of the redeemed.

Then "they found God somehow inside them as well: directing them, making them able to do things they could not do before. And when they worked it all out they found they had arrived at the Christian definition of the three-personal God." Consequently, even if unfamiliar with the Trinitarian formulation, they were well acquainted with its practical application.

This, in turn, recalls a telephone conversation with an orthodox Jewish rabbi. At one point, he unexpectedly blurted out: " It is inconceivable that Jews would hold to the doctrine of the Trinity!"

"In the sense that they were not involved in the creedal affirmation," I allowed. "However, it is obvious that the Christian faith first appealed in Jewish circles. Perhaps they viewed Jesus along the line of a Messianic Theophany."

"Well," he replied, "that would certainly be Jewish. It would explain why some believed in him, and others of us do not." Whereupon, he turned to other matters.

This interchange invites us to look at the Jewish tradition more closely. It is common knowledge that the Hebrew faith is monotheistic. As expressed in the *shema*, "Hear, O Israel: The Lord our God, the Lord is one. Love the Lord your God with all your heart and with all your soul and with all your strength" (Deut. 6:4-5). The term *shema* is derived from the first word in the initial verse, the admonition to *hear*.

The *shema* serves both as a foundational truth and a resulting obligation. Since God is one, he is deserving of our undivided devotion. As sometimes expressed, love God and do as you please; for if you genuinely love God, you will do as he pleases.

This, moreover, brings to mind an extended discussion among another Christian, myself, and four Muslims: a religious judge, retired academic professor, lecturer, and merchant—who graciously hosted the meeting. The retired professor was first to speak. "Now the doctrine of the Trinity," he noted. "This should not concern us. While I cannot embrace the orthodox Christian teaching, the matter of complexity in the Godhead is quite acceptable."

The continuing importance of complex monotheism in Jewish tradition can best be explained in terms of God dwelling among his people. For instance, "Then have them make a sanctuary for me, and I will dwell among them" (Exod. 25:8). For another, "Why gaze in envy, O rugged mountains, at the mountains where God chooses to reign, where the Lord himself will dwell forever?" (Psa. 68:16).

The term *shekinah* is a transliteration of the Hebrew word meaning *the one who dwells*. It came to be used to describe the immanent presence in the world of a transcendent deity. While the word itself is not employed in the New Testament, the notion carries over. As an example, "The Word became flesh and made his dwelling among us. We have seen his glory, the glory of the One and Only, who came from the Father, full of grace and truth" (John 1:14). Then, in anticipation of his ascension, Jesus promised his disciples: "And I will ask the Father, and he will give you another Counselor to be with you forever—the Spirit of truth" (John 14:16-17).

The Christian adaptation of complex monotheism both draws from its Jewish antecedent, and accommodates it to the advent of Jesus as the Messiah. These alike assume that God takes the initiative to recover man from his waywardness. Jesus likens this to a shepherd who leaves his flock to search for the sheep which was lost. Upon recovering the prized animal, he rejoices with his friends.

The Christian also shares the Hebraic conviction that God progressively reveals himself. Revelation may be said to resemble a seed that after it germinates, thrusts out its roots and breaks the ground with a tender sprout. It eventually grows a sturdy trunk, and several branches adorn it with copious leaves. All this comes to fruition when buds burst forth into exotic blossoms. In more succinct terms, "In times past God spoke to our forefathers through the prophets at many times and in various ways, but in these last days he has spoken to us by his Son" (Heb. 1:1-2).

In this connection, Jesus assured his listeners: "Do not think that I have come to abolish the Law or the Prophets; I have not come to abolish them but to fulfill them" (Matt. 5:17). As for pointed commentary, "Jesus did not come to do away with the Law and the Prophets but to bring out by word and deed the quality of life they were intended to produce."[2]

I find it helpful to think of the advent of Jesus as the Messiah in terms of a *paradigm shift*. The term *paradigm* might otherwise be expressed as a model or construct. Lord Kelvin confidently commented in 1900, "there is nothing new to be discovered in physics. All that remains is more and more precise measurement." Only five years later, Albert Einstein published his paper on special relativity, which dramatically altered the way we understand the world in which we live.

According to Thomas Kuhn, "Successive transition from one paradigm to another is the usual development of mature science."[3] He was not assured that the notion of paradigm shifts could be applied as readily in the Social Sciences.

Initially, there is a growing awareness that the current paradigm will not handle all the known events. This characteristically results in tentative efforts to explain the phenomena more accurately. As a matter of record, messianic expectation was building during the period leading up to birth of Jesus. A number of persons laid claim to being the Messiah. In retrospect, "Some time ago Theudas appeared claiming to be somebody, and about four hundred men rallied to him. He was killed, all his followers were dispersed, and it all came to nothing. After, Judas the Galilean appeared in the days of the census, and led a band of people in revolt" (Acts 5:36-37). He was also killed, and his followers scattered. Gamaliel, consequently, urges his associates to let the Jesus movement run its course, since "if it is from God, you will not be able to stop these men; you will only find yourselves fighting against God."

The hint of a paradigm shift solicits predictable resistance, especially among those who have the most to benefit by maintaining the status quo. So it was that the religious hierarchy concluded that Jesus must be done away with, although not in a precipitous manner—for fear of offending the populace.

Moreover,

> The Messianic portrait remained ambiguous, due to seemingly contradictory ingredients, accentuated by personal and corporate preference. On the one hand, it appeared as if God Himself would intervene; on the other, as if through a chosen agent. On the one hand, the Messiah appeared as a military figure, on the other, as a heavenly agent. On the one hand, as the royal heir to David's throne; on the other, as a suffering servant.[4]

The royal aspect, nonetheless, dominated.

Once the new paradigm emerges, it is necessary to refine its implications. In this regard, Jesus' disciples approached him with the petition: "Tell us, when will this (the destruction of the temple) happen, and what will be the sign of your coming and of the end of the age?" (Matt. 24:3).

Jesus cautioned them in response: "Watch out that no one deceives you. For many will come in my name, claiming, 'I am the Christ,' and will deceive many. You will hear of wars and rumors of wars, but see to it that you are not alarmed." Such things must come to pass, but the end is yet to come. "Nation will rise against nation, and kingdom against kingdom. There will be famines and earthquakes in various places. All these are the beginning of birth pains." He continued to speak to them along these lines concerning the time leading up to the consummation of the age.

"So when you see standing in the holy place the abomination that causes desolation, then let those who are in Judea flee to the mountains." *The abomination that causes desolation* finds "its origin in that critical period that gave rise to the Maccabean revolution, and then to understand that it has surfaced in history whenever the purposes of God have been violently assaulted by the forces of evil."[5] Consequently, it appears that Christians fled at the sign of the approaching pagan forces, to find sanctuary in the Trans-Jordan.

As noted above, the religious hierarchy was determined that Jesus must be eliminated. He was apprehended and whisked off for a hasty interrogation before the High Priest. Afterward, he was brought before the Roman official Pilate. When he could find nothing countenancing execution, Pilate proposed to release Jesus after scourging. Incidently, this in itself could result in death.

The populace, at the instigation of the Jewish officials, insisted that Jesus be crucified. Pilate yielded to their demands, so as to preserve the Pax Romana. So it was that they crucified Jesus, along with two common criminals. The religious establishment heaved a collective sigh of relief.

Its consolation was short-lived. Women who made their way to Jesus' tomb to anoint his body found it empty. "Suddenly two men in clothes that gleamed like lightning stood beside them" (Luke 24:4). "Why do you look for the living among the dead?" they inquired. "He is not here; he is risen!"

Subsequently, Jesus appeared to his disciples over an extended period of forty days. They were amazed, consoled, and perplexed. "Lord," they inquired of him, "are you at this time going to restore the kingdom to Israel? (Acts 1:6).

He replied, "It is not for you to know the times or dates the Father has set by his own authority. But you will receive power when the Holy Spirit comes on you, and you will be my witnesses in Jerusalem, and in all Judea and Samaria, and to the ends of the earth." In particular, their calling would involve obedience, service, and suffering. "Obedience first, since it was in response to Jesus' injunction; service second, because it requires putting the welfare of others above that of themselves, suffering last, in that Christ calls his disciples to take up their cross and follow him."[6]

Upon the occasion of Pentecost, they were assembled—when suddenly a sound like the blowing of a violent wind came from heaven, and filled the house where they were sitting. They also saw what seemed to be tongues of fire that separated and came to rest on each of them. Accordingly, they were all filled with the Holy Spirit, and some or all began to speak with other tongues—as the Spirit enabled them. As noted in an earlier context, this resembled previous theophanies—as illustrated at Sinai.

The expression *filled with the Spirit* is employed here with reference to their initial experience, and then on subsequent occasions (cf. Acts 4:8, 31; 13:9). We are thus alerted to the fact "that a person already filled with the Spirit can receive a fresh filling for a specific task, or a continuous filling. . . . The basic act of receiving the Spirit can be described as being baptized or filled, but the verb 'baptize' is not used for subsequent experiences."[7] As such, baptism of the Spirit is comparable to water baptism.

Other tongues could be a reference to ecstatic utterance, alternative languages, or some combination of the two. Since persons heard them speaking in their own dialects, it would appear to rule out the first option. Perhaps significant is the fact that persons can subconsciously retain catches of another language, and give expression to them when emotionally excited.

In any case, the outpouring of the Spirit is associated with Jesus' intercession, and for the purpose of fulfilling the great commission. It would seem to follow that the prime evidence for being filled with the Spirit would be the commitment to disciple all nations. Conversely, it is instrumental in bonding believers together in a common task.

All things considered, this paradoxical mystery refuses to be put to rest. In retrospect, "This was the first doctrine really to captivate the church. Even the disputes about the person of Christ were initially a function of the issue."[8] It was simply considered too important a concern to ignore.

As a result, a succession of councils were called, each to refine the church's position more precisely. An incredible amount of time and energy were expended in the process. According to one graphic and amusing report, "The roads were filled with traveling bishops."

Not to be overlooked, these efforts were largely successful in setting aside two contrasting and unacceptable alternatives. On the one hand, it repudiated tritheism, or for that matter any other form of polytheism. On the other, it set up a stalwart defense against modalism. In particular, the suggestion that the one God merely employs three different roles or modes. First, as Creator; then, as Redeemer; finally, so as to enable the recipients of God's grace.

"Beyond that, however, this was a discussion that had far-reaching political implications. The Roman emperors realized that with the close connection between the church and the imperial government a doctrinal schism . . . had the potential of splitting the empire asunder."[9] Thus the doctrinal struggle spilled over into public affairs; and, in turn, left its mark on secular history.

3

THE INCARNATION

The *incarnation* is succinctly expressed by way of "the Word became flesh" (John 1:14). Paul elaborates in greater detail by getting a running start, "Your attitude should be the same as that of Christ Jesus: Who being in very nature God, did not consider equality with God something to be grasped, but emptied himself, taking on the nature of a servant, being made in human likeness" (Phil. 2:5-7). Whereupon, he became obedient unto death.

It seems remarkable that a practical issue would give rise to what some would assert is the most profound theological pronouncement in Scripture. Paul appeals to his readers that they defer to others, rather than further their own agenda. In other words, to assume the role of a servant.

Jesus is set forth as the prime example. Although by virtue of being divine, he did not insist on maintaining its prerogatives— so as to accomplish his redemptive mission. It goes without saying that he did not compromise his essential nature. Conversely, he no longer exercised such features as omnipotence or omniscience. As for the latter, "No one knows about that day or hour, not even the angels in heaven, nor the Son, but only the Father" (Mark 13:32).

In doing so, Jesus took on human nature, with one critical exception. In this regard, "For we do not have a high priest who is unable to sympathize with our weaknesses, but we have one who has been tempted in every way, just as we are—yet was without sin" (Heb. 4:15). "The full humanity of Jesus means that he experienced the full range (rather than every specific manifestation) of human temptation, although to a much higher degree of intensity since, unlike all others, he never yielded to sin."[1] This serves as a reminder that temptation is heightened in the face of resolute resistance.

"And being found in appearance as a man," the apostle continues, "he humbled himself and became obedient to death—even death on a cross!" "The whole composition celebrates Jesus' humiliation, and his humiliation was crowned by his undergoing **death on a cross**. By the standards of the first century, no experience could be more loathsomely degrading than that."[2]

Now it came to pass that God sent the angel Gabriel to Nazareth in the Galilee, to a virgin pledge to be married to a man named *Joseph*—who was of the lineage of David. Her name was *Mary*. "Greetings," the angel addressed her, "you who are highly favored! The Lord is with you" (Luke 1:28). "You will be with child and give birth to a son," he continued, "and you are to give him the name Jesus." Although a common name, it was well suited to his redemptive role.

"How can this be," Mary asked in astonishment, "since I am a virgin?"

The angel replied: "The Holy Spirit will come upon you, and the power of the Most High will over-shadow you. So the holy one to be born will be called the Son of God." While Mary will be instrumental in the birth, the accent is placed on the divine involvement. Moreover, "This delicate expression rules out crude ideas of a 'mating' of the Holy Spirit with Mary."[3]

"My soul glorifies the Lord and my spirit rejoices in God my Savior," Mary enthused, "for he has been mindful of the humble state of his servant. From now on all generations will call me blessed, for the Mighty One has done great things for me—holy is his name." After this, she explores God's blessings in more general terms.

In the course of time, there was a census requiring that Joseph register in Bethlehem, since he was descended from David. Mary, now well advanced in her pregnancy, accompanied him. While they were there, she gave birth.

Now there were shepherds living out in the fields nearby, keeping watch over their flocks at night. An angel appeared to them, and the glory of the Lord shone around them—so that they were terrified. "Do not be afraid," the angel assured him, "I bring you good news of great joy that will be for all the people. Today in the town of David a Savior has been born to you; he is Christ the Lord."

Suddenly a great company of the heavenly host appeared with the angel, praising God and saying: "Glory to God in the highest, and on earth peace to men on whom his favor rests." *Glory to God in the highest* and *on earth peace to men on whom his favor rests* resemble two sides of a coin. Consequently, the shepherds are invited to join in the acclaim of God for the peace that will ensue.

"Now Jesus was about thirty years old when he began his ministry" (Luke 3:23). This is by way of suggesting that he had reached a proper age for public service (cf. Gen. 41:46; Num. 4:3, 23; 2 Sam. 5:4). Earlier on, he would have assisted Joseph. Furthermore, some speculate that Joseph passed away during the interim, so that Jesus assumed responsibility for the welfare of his family.

Jesus returned to Galilee from the wilderness, and he taught in the synagogues. In this context, he went to Nazareth where he was brought up, and made his way to the synagogue—as was his custom. He stood up to read, and the Isaiah scroll was handed to him. Unrolling it, he found the place where it is written: "The Spirit of the Lord is on me, because he has anointed me to preach good news to the poor. He has sent me to proclaim freedom for the prisoners and recovery of sight for the blind, to release the oppressed, to proclaim the year of the Lord's favor" (Luke 4:18-19; cf. Isa. 61:1-2). This employed Jubilee imagery associated with the Messianic Age.

He then rolled up the scroll, handed it back to the attendant, and sat down—in anticipation of teaching. The eyes of everyone were fixed upon him, as he began by saying: "Today this scripture is fulfilled in your hearing."

All were favorably disposed toward him, and were amazed at the gracious words. "Isn't this Joseph's son?" they inquired. "The positive response to Jesus by his audience within the synagogue was based on a narrow, provincial understanding of his identity and mission. It is as though to this juncture they have filtered his message through their restrictive presumptions about him."[4] In particular, there is no indication that they thought of him as out of the ordinary.

It remained for a later generation to credit Jesus with remarkable and even bizarre activity as a child. For instance, Joseph was said to have received an order from a rich man to make a bed for him. When one board turned out to be shorter than another, Joseph did not know what to do about the situation. "Put the two boards down and line them up at one end," Jesus instructed him. Whereupon, Jesus took hold of the shorter board and stretched it, so that it was the same length.

Joseph embraced the child, observing: "How fortunate I am that God has given this child to me."[5] Thus concluding an episode quite alien to the biblical text.

Jesus seems to have intuitively realized what those in attendance were thinking. "Surely you will quote this proverb to me: 'Physician heal yourself!'" he exclaimed. "'Do here in your home town what we have heard that you did in Capernaum.'"

"I tell you the truth," he solemnly continued, "no prophet is accepted in his home-town. I assure you that there were many widows in Israel in Elijah's time . . . yet (he) was not sent to any of them, but to the widow in Zarephath in the region of Sidon." And there were many in Israel during the time of Elisha, but none of them were cleansed—only Naaman the Syrian. "Jesus' status is (thus) certified, first, by the relation of his ministry to theirs and then by the fact that, like prophets of old, he is rejected."[6]

All the people were furious with him. They got to their feet, drove him out of town, and took him to the brow of a hill—to throw him off the cliff. However, he walked through the crowd and went on his way. "He simply walked through the mob. Some have felt that this was itself a miracle—though not the kind of miracle the Nazarenes wanted."[7]

Then he went down to Capernaum, located by the shore of the Sea of Galilee and sitting astride one branch of the Via Maris international trade route. It was by way of the imposing Arbel Pass, where Zealots would from time to time hide in the overlooking cliffs. Armies had taken that way previously, bent on conquest or intending to address some wrong. Now Jesus travels this way, along with his rag-tag group of followers.

This, in turn, brings to mind the classic text *One Solitary Life*, best quoted at some length.

Here is a young man who was born in an obscure village, the child of a peasant woman. He worked in a carpenter shop until age 30 and then for three years He was an itinerant teacher. He never wrote a book. He never went to college. He never traveled more than 200 miles from the place where He was born. He never did one of the things that usually accompany greatness. He had no credential other than Himself. . . . Nineteen centuries have come and gone and today, He is the central figure of the human race and the leader of the column of progress.

"They were amazed at his teaching, because his message had authority." Originality was not highly prized among the rabbis, who characteristically accredited their teaching by citing illustrious predecessors. Jesus dared to be different, because he was different from the rest.

There was in the synagogue a demoniac. "Ha!" he cried at the top of his voice, "What is it that you want from us, Jesus of Nazareth? Have you come to destroy us? I know who you are—the Holy One of God!" He thus recognizes Jesus as an adversary, not unlike C. S. Lewis' colorful demonic character *Screwtape*, who warns his nephew *Wormwood*: "The Enemy will be working from the center outwards, gradually bringing more and more of the patient's conduct under the new standard, and may reach his behavior to the old lady at any moment. You want to get in first."[8]

"Be quiet!" Jesus sternly rebuked him. "Come out of him!" At this, the demon threw the man down, without injuring him. All the people were amazed and inquired among themselves: "What is this teaching? With authority and power he gives orders to evil spirits and they come out!" Accordingly, he backed up his authoritative teaching with commensurate performance—so that the word was spread throughout the whole region.

Incidently, miracles are not uniformly attributed in Scripture to great personages. John the Baptist serves as a prime example. While portrayed as a critical component in salvation history, he is credited with no miracles.

"In the sayings of Jesus as found in the Gospels we encounter again and again that phrase of revelation: 'I am He.' Perhaps this phrase harbors within itself the most authentic, the most audacious, and the most profound affirmation by Jews of who he was."[9] As assessed later, "'I am He'—this meant: where I am there God is, there God lives and speaks, calls, asks, acts, decides, loves, chooses, forgives, rejects, suffers and dies. Nothing bolder can be said, or imagined."

Standing over against this confluence of the extraordinary is Jesus' forthright humanity. Now Jesus was on his way back to Galilee, when he and his disciples arrived at Jacob's well. Tired from the journey, (he) sat down by the well—while his disciples went to town to buy food (cf. John 4:6). Consequently, he appears exhausted.

On another occasion, "From this time many of his disciples turned back and no longer followed him" (John 6:65). "You do not want to leave too, do you?" Jesus plaintively inquired of the Twelve. He appears deeply hurt by the defection of others, and hopes that it will not extend to these as well.

"Lord," Simon Peter heartily responded, "to whom shall we go? You have the words of eternal life. We believe and know that you are the Holy One of God." Jesus was doubtless pleased, even though one would betray him and another deny him.

On still another occasion, Lazarus was critically ill. Upon the arrival of Jesus and his disciples, they found that their friend had been in the tomb for four days. When Jesus saw his sister Mary and the others weeping, he was deeply moved. "Where have you laid him?" he empathetically inquired (John 11:34).

"Come and see, Lord," they replied.

Jesus, in turn, wept; in a very human manner—rather than immune from the sorrows that plague our existence. This was before he restored Lazarus to life, and reunited him with his family.

The time of Jesus' demise was fast approaching. He went out as usual to the Mount of Olives, and his disciples followed him. Upon reaching the place, he admonished them: "Pray that you will not fall into temptation" (Luke 22:40). After this, he withdrew about a stone's throw, and intently prayed: "Father, if you are willing, take this cup from me; yet not my will, but yours be done." An angel appeared in response to his petition. And being in anguish, he prayed more earnestly, and his sweat was like drops of blood falling to the ground. It must have seemed as if the weight of the world was on his shoulders, and in a manner of speaking, it was!

The ordeal of scourging and crucifixion still awaited him. As for the former, it was graphically called *the half-way death*. It usually consisted of thirty-nine lashes, but could be extended—depending on the mood of those applying the punishment. "The soldier would use a whip of braided leather thongs with metal balls woven into them. When the whip would strike the flesh, these balls would cause deep bruises or contusions, which would break open with further blows."[10] Alternatively, the whip might have pieces of sharp bone as well.

As for the latter, once a person is stretched on a cross, crucifixion is characteristically an agonizing slow death by asphyxiation. "After managing to exhale, the person would then be able to relax down and take another breath in. Again he'd have to push himself up to exhale. This would go on and on until complete exhaustion would take over."[11] All things considered, Jesus probed the depth of human pathos.

Later speculation was tempted to go to extremes by accenting Jesus' divinity to the virtual exclusion of his humanity—as with Docetism, or the reverse—as with the Ebionites. While manifestly both must be kept in delicate balance.

4

ILLUSIVE MYSTERY

"The wind blows wherever it pleases," Jesus observed. "You hear its sound, but you cannot tell where it comes from or where it is going. So it is with everyone born of the Spirit" (John 3:8). The term for *wind* and *Spirit* being the same, it provides for a convenient play on words.

The imagery is quite familiar. One might be sitting on the front porch, and the air is still. There is no perceptible movement in the branches of the surrounding trees. Suddenly, inexplicably, there is rustling of the leaves—as a gust of wind disturbs the tranquility. This lasts for only a fleeting moment, before silence returns. This is graphically illustrative of the illusive activity of the Spirit.

It serves to get a running start from a series of vantage points from which we can view salvation history. Sinai first invites our attention. "The traditional site for Mount Sinai is a granite ridge, the peaks of which reach about 8,000 feet above sea level. The most conspicuous peak, Jebel Musa (Mountain of Moses), looks out toward a wide plain approximately four miles in length and up to a mile in width."[1] According to tradition, it was here that the Israelites assembled, and Moses received on their behalf a gracious covenant with the Almighty.

It was also in this context that creation was recalled. "In the beginning God created the heavens and the earth," the narrative is solemnly introduced. "Now the earth was formless and empty, darkness was over the surface of the deep, and the Spirit of God was hovering over the waters" (Gen. 1:1-2). "While not inviting, chaos appears as if the first step in the creative process. As such, it is similar to many other High God traditions. These resemble the potter who casts his clay before refining it into a vessel for use."[2]

According to an alternative tradition, creation resembles whittling a stick so as to fashion an object. This, in turn, recalls a gifted individual who could carve an amazing portrait in wood. He was of the opinion that there was something inherent in the material that made this possible.

Time rapidly passes. We deftly shift our attention from the mountain of God to the gates of Zion. One generation has perished in the wilderness, while the next has succeeded in entering the promised land. The turbulent era of the Judges has intervened, during which God raised up leaders to provide the people with relief from oppression. As an example, "The Spirit of the Lord came upon him (Othniel), so that he became Israel's judge and he went to war. The Lord gave Cushan-Rishathaim, king of Aram into the hands of Othniel, who overpowered him. So the land had peace for forty years" (Judges 3:10-11).

The people subsequently petitioned Samuel to appoint a king over them, although he was reluctant to comply with their wishes. "Listen to the voice of the people in regard to all that they say to you," the Lord prompted him, "for they have not rejected you, but they have rejected Me from being king over them" (1 Sam. 8:7).

Prophetic activity flourished with the monarchy. The prophets assumed the uninviting task of fine-tuning the monarchy to its covenant obligations. In retrospect, "For prophecy never had its origin in the will of man, but men spoke from God as they were carried along by the Holy Spirit" (2 Peter 1:21). If *carried along*, then something more dynamic than simple dictation.

Time does not stand still. The early rulers began well, but faltered with the passing of time. The Northern Kingdom went into a tight spiral, from which there was no recovery. The Southern Kingdom fared better, but eventually succumbed. The Israelites endured exile in anticipation of a promised deliverer.

"No better vantage point exists for us to survey the saga of the Spirit than Calvary. Here Christ died to redeem man from his sin, and from here we gain perspective on all the rest."[3] As if to confirm this thesis, an angel informed Mary: "The Holy Spirit will come upon you. So the holy one to be born will be called the Son of God" (Luke 1:35).

"The rabbis observed that while some choose to cooperate with God's gracious purpose, others fail to do so. Even so, God keeps them on a short leash. Then, in the end, God's will must triumph. So it would appear when factoring the Spirit into life's equation."[4]

The coming of the Messiah was expectantly anticipated. Now Simeon was a devout person, who "was waiting for the consolation of Israel, and the Holy Spirit was upon him" (Luke 2:25). The *coming* was a major feature in Hebrew tradition, calling for a pious response, and preceded by what would graphically resemble travail. Consequently, the Holy Spirit appears as an agent of consolation.

In context, "It had been revealed to him by the Holy Spirit that he would not die before he had seen the Lord's Christ. Moved by the Spirit, he went into the temple courts." Upon seeing the child Jesus, Simeon took him in his arms, praising God, saying: "Sovereign Lord, as you have promised, you now dismiss your servant in peace. For my eyes have seen your salvation, which you have prepared in the sight of all people, a light for revelation to the Gentiles and for glory to your people Israel." This convergence of events is portrayed as resulting from the activity of the Spirit.

John the Baptist subsequently came preaching "a baptism of repentance for the forgiveness of sin" (Luke 3:3). Jesus also came to be baptized. As he was praying, "heaven was opened and the Holy Spirit descended on him in bodily form like a dove. And a voice came from heaven, 'You are my Son, whom I love; with you I am well pleased.'" Luke reveals less interest in Jesus' baptism as such than "his endowment with the Spirit and God's affirmation of his sonship. . . . The initial dependent clauses lead into the focal point of this pericope by stressing Jesus' solidarity with those who had responded positively to John's message."[5] As such, he readily identifies with those he will redeem.

In particular, the Spirit is portrayed as anointing Jesus for his redemptive ministry. In this regard, we are reminded that the *dove* served as a sacrifice. Then, too, it was a harbinger of *shalom* (peace, well-being).

"Jesus, full of the Holy Spirit, returned from the Jordan and was led by the Spirit in the desert, where for forty days he was tempted by the devil" (Luke 4:1). The order is likely significant, in that to be led by the Spirit one must be filled. While the temptations can be viewed from a number of perspectives, the most plausible is in terms of his messianic resolve.

Jesus returned to Galilee in the power of the Spirit, and news concerning him spread through the region (cf. Luke 4:14). I take this to mean that he was invigorated by the Spirit, which led him to declare the message persuasively, and persist in the face of opposition and trying circumstances.

"I must preach the good news of the kingdom of God," he explained to his listeners (v. 43). This constituted the burden of his ministry. "The expression (Kingdom of God) summarizes the hopes and dreams of Jesus' Jewish contemporaries who longed for the fulfillment of the Old Testament prophecies which spoke of a return of a golden era to Israel."[6] Not that Israel was the only beneficiary, because these had universal implications.

As if to summarize, Jesus quoted a text from Isaiah: "The Spirit of the Lord is on me, because he has anointed me to preach good news" (v. 18). The Spirit is thus cast in the already familiar role of a divine facilitator.

Jesus' life and ministry did not deviate from his expressed purpose. "As the time approached for him to be taken up to heaven, Jesus resolutely set out for Jerusalem" (Luke 9:51). Along the way, he warned his disciples of the cost of discipleship. Once, when certain disciples reported back to him, he—being *full of joy through the Holy Spirit*—acknowledged the Father for having hidden these truths from the learned, and revealing them to little children (cf. Luke 10:21). "What is revealed to them, then, is a major Lukan concern—namely, that (1) the dominion of God is historically present in the redemptive activity of Jesus and (2) thus, also in the activity of Jesus' emissaries who act (and may, like him, encounter rejection) 'in his name.'"[7]

Jesus' days are numbered. He retires to Gethsemane, along with his disciples. Having urged them to keep a prayer vigil, he withdrew a stone's throw beyond them. "Father," he petitioned, "if you are willing, take this cup from me; yet not my will, but yours be done" (Luke 22:42). This was in keeping with the whole tenor of his ministry, as orchestrated by the Spirit.

In the stirring lyrics of Robert Lowry:

Death cannot keep his prey—Jesus my Savior,
he tore the bars away—Jesus my Lord!
Up from the grave he arose, with a mighty triumph over his foes;
he arose a victor from the dark domain, and he lives forever with his saints to reign.
He arose! He arose! Hallelujah! Christ arose!

In retrospect, Luke acknowledges that his initial volume concerned "all that Jesus began to do and to teach until the day he was taken up to heaven, after giving instructions through the Holy Spirit to the apostles he had chosen" (Acts 1:1-2). Jesus had chosen the apostles as his emissaries, while the Spirit served as their mentor.

"Do not leave Jerusalem," Jesus had admonished his disciples, "but wait for the gift my Father promised." Within "a few days you will be baptized with the Holy Spirit." As mentioned in a previous context, this was associated with Jesus' Ascension. Luke would have us understand that he thus continues his instructive role, but under different circumstances.

The account concerning the outpouring of the Holy Spirit need not concern us, since it was considered in a prior context. More central to the discussion is a thesis argued on another occasion: "I suggest that the book of Acts represents the community of faith as the prime manifestation of the Holy Spirit. I am further convinced, although I shall not attempt to labor the point at this time, that the gospel of Luke is consistent with this conclusion."[8] Mention of this was made in forty of forty-eight episodes related in Acts concerning the manifestation of the illusive Spirit.

This community is characterized in a number of ways. As mentioned earlier, it embraced as a corporate task to disciple the nations. Each person, having made his or her way to the cross, encountered others in a life of service.

As Luke implies at the outset of his second volume, this fellowship was apostolic in its orientation. By way of confirmation, "They devoted themselves to the apostles' teaching" (Acts 2:42). The remaining characteristics would be derivative.

Not only is the church apostolic, but one. This may not appear to be the case, considering the many overt divisions. However, it was baptized into one body, and sustained by the same Spirit. Its unity should not be confused with uniformity, but more resembles a constructive diversity.

The church is no less holy. Not that it is without blame, but in that God has summoned it for his purpose. As such, it is in continuing need of repentance and restoration. In this regard, "For it is time for judgment to begin with the family of God, and if it begins with us, what will the outcome be for those who do not obey the gospel of God?" (1 Peter 4:17).

Finally, the church is catholic or universal. A proper balance must be kept in this regard. On the one hand, every culture provides a means through which the gospel may be proclaimed. On the other, there is no culture so pristine but that it will not come under the critique of Holy Writ.

"Luke prompts us to consider community in more concrete terms. In particular, he makes reference 'to the breaking of bread and prayer.' *The breaking of bread* could be associated with a common meal or the Lord's Supper, although the two are likely combined."[9] Worthy of note, the common meal constituted the simplest form of a covenant expression in antiquity.

It is common knowledge that Luke accents prayer at critical moments in his two-volume narrative. Whether concerning the life and ministry of Jesus, or in connection with the activity of his followers. This, in turn, alerts us to the fact that the Spirit ministers in and through our earnest petitions.

Signs and wonders are not exclusively but primarily associated with the apostles. These become a means of authenticating their ministry, as was the case with Jesus. Even then, they were sometimes misunderstood. As an example, when the Lyconians witnessed the healing of a cripple, they cried out: "The gods have come down to us in human form!" (Acts 14:11).

When Paul and Barnabas heard of this, they protested: "We too are only men, human like you. We are bringing you good news, telling you to turn from these worthless things to the living God, who made heaven and earth, and sea and everything in them." In spite of this, they had difficulty in keeping the populace from offering sacrifice to them. Only to have the populace turn against them, when instigators incited them to reprisal.

"All the believers were together and had everything in common. Selling their possessions and goods, they gave to anyone as he had need" (Acts 2:44-45). As it is shortly made clear, this was not incumbent on persons—nor can it be taken as normative for the Christian fellowship. Conversely, it provides evidence for the generous spirit of those cultivated by the Spirit.

While the subtle working of the Spirit can be illustrated in various other ways, the preceding will suffice. He as a rule serves in a subtle manner, so as not to call undue attention to himself. Hence, to forge the bonds of fellowship, and extend the ministry of Christian outreach. All things considered, he qualifies as *the illusive mystery*.

5

RUMOR OF ANGELS

Angels are incorporeal. However, they can appear in human form, sometimes radiating light. They may have the suggestion of wings, accenting its role as an emissary of the Almighty.

Now that the pump is primed, we turn to a classic instance. "One day the angels came to present themselves before the Lord, and Satan also came with them" (Job. 1:6). God is portrayed as the universal sovereign, to whom all are responsible. This includes a heavenly host, as well as humans. Satan proves not to be an exception. We are thus alerted to the fact that God keeps evil on a short leash.

"Where do you come from?" the sovereign inquired of Satan—as if to require an accounting.

Satan evasively replied, "From roaming through the earth and going back and forth in it."

"Have you seen my servant Job?" the sovereign pointedly inquired. "There is no one on earth like him; he is blameless and upright, a man who fears God and shuns evil." "Righteous men are rare. It may be hard to find a few (Gen. 18:22-33) or even one (Jer. 5:1) in a city. But it is possible; and when the Lord observes a good man, He is delighted (Isa. 42:1)."[1]

"Does Job fear God for nothing?" Satan impugned. "Have you not put a hedge around him and his household and everything he has? But stretch out your hand and strike everything he has, and he will surely curse you to your face." "Cynicism is the essence of the satanic. Satan believes nothing to be genuinely good—neither Job in his disinterested piety nor God in His disinterested generosity."[2] Otherwise expressed, the satanic is void of hope.

"Very well," God agreed—in terms of what is usually described as his *permissive will*. In other words, he allows that which does not as such please him. Yet, with the realization that all things work together for good for those who are genuinely devout (cf. Rom. 8:28).

In the end, the patriarch was exonerated. He was rewarded in part by the privilege to intercede on behalf of his insensitive friends. Then, too, "The Lord blessed the latter part of Job's life more than the first" (42:12)—with family, possessions, and long life.

Initially, Eliphaz rhetorically inquires, "if he (God) charges his angels with error, how much more those who live in houses of clay" (4:18). While correct in his assessment, he proves to be simplistic in his solution.

Subsequently, Elihu allows, "if there is an angel on his side as a mediator to tell a man what is right for him then his flesh is renewed like a child's" (33:23, 25). Such a person is indeed fortunate to have the error of his ways pointed out. Moreover, it is incumbent on him or her to heed the angel's counsel.

All things considered, we are given the impression that there are angels ministering in our midst. They are as a rule well-meaning, as divine emissaries. There are unfortunately exceptions, with Satan proving to be the prime culprit. These are depicted as having fallen from divine favor, and bent on frustrating God's benevolent purposes.

In greater detail, after God had ejected Adam and Eve from paradise, he stationed cherubim with a flaming sword to guard the way to the tree of life (cf. Gen. 3:24). "Only here in the OT do the cherubim engage in police activity. All OT references to the cherubim suggest, directly or indirectly, that the cherubim are symbols of God's presence."[3] They resemble a chariot (cf. 2 Sam. 22:1), thus accommodating the Almighty (cf. 1 Sam. 4:4; Psa. 80:2).

It is for fortuitous purposes that the duo is barred from access to the tree of life, lest they perpetuate their alienation indefinitely. Meanwhile, salvation history must run its course. The tree of life awaits the pilgrim's arduous journey to the celestial city (cf. Rev. 22:2).

We are well-advised to be selective in the treatment of angels, because they show up frequently in the biblical narratives. "Take your son, your only son, Isaac, whom you love, and go to the region of Moriah," God enjoined Abraham. "Sacrifice him there as a burnt offering on one of the mountains I will tell you about" (Gen. 22:2). While child sacrifice was a common phenomenon in pagan culture, this was not in keeping with the Almighty's high regard for life. Then, too, it was through Isaac that God's promises would be realized. In retrospect, "Abraham reasoned that God could raise the dead, and figuratively speaking he did receive Isaac back from death" (Heb. 11:19).

So when the patriarch lifted his knife to slay the boy, an angel called out to him from heaven: "Do not lay a hand on the boy. Do not do anything to him. For I know that you fear God, because you have not withheld from me your son, your only son." After which, the Almighty provided a welcome substitute.

This topic allows us to revisit some instances touched on earlier. As an example, Moses was tending his father-in-law's flock in the vicinity of the *Mountain of God*. "There the angel of the Lord appeared to him in flames of fire from within a bush" (Exod. 3:2). First, it should be noted that the angel of the Lord provides the most characteristic form of revelation during the patriarchal period (cf. Gen. 16:7; 22:11, 15; 24:7, 40; 31:11; 48:16).

Second, the angel distinguishes himself from the Almighty—by speaking of Him in the third person; while on the other hand, he identifies with God—by speaking in the first person. This has given rise to various speculative theories that need not concern us. Suffice to say, the angel of the Lord underscores God's presence—as a comfort to the righteous and a warning to the callous. In this connection, "The angel of the Lord encamps around those who fear him, and he delivers them" (Psa. 34:7).

Concerning another previously mentioned example, Isaiah "saw the Lord seated on a throne, high and exalted, and the train of his robe filled the temple. Above him were seraphs, each with six wings. With two wings they covered their faces, with two they covered their feet, and with two they were flying" (Isa. 6:1-2).

Meanwhile, they were calling out to one another: "Holy, holy, holy is the Lord Almighty; the whole earth is full of his glory."

Subsequently, one of the seraphs flew to Isaiah with a live coal in his hand, which he had taken with tongs from the altar. "See," he enjoined the prophet, "this has touched your lips, your guilt is taken away and your sin atoned for." The seraphim are mentioned only in this connection. From the scant evidence available, we can conclude that they were occupied continually with the praise and adoration of the sovereign deity. God also seems to have delegated them certain responsibilities.

The exile was an especially traumatic experience for the Israelites. The beloved City of the Great King lay in ruin. The more privileged class was whisked away to unfamiliar surroundings, leaving the landed poor to struggle with a social structure in chaos. To the degree that they felt culpable, guilt must have weighed heavily upon them.

While in captivity, Daniel had a vision of one "dressed in linen, with a belt of the finest gold around his waist. His body was like chrysolite, his face like lightning, his eyes like flaming torches, his arms and legs like the gleam of burnished bronze, and his voice like the sound of a multitude" (10:5-6). It was a heavenly messenger (cf. v. 11).

"Do not be afraid," the visitor encouraged Daniel. "Since the first day that you set your mind to gain understanding and to humble yourself before your God, your words were heard, (but) the prince of the Persian kingdom resisted me for twenty-one days. Then Michael, one of the chief princes, came to help me."

These princes appear to be angelic patrons, Greece also having a counterpart (cf. v. 20), while "Michael, *one of the chief princes*, belongs to Israel. Evidently the hierarchy in the heavenlies is not a replica of that on earth, where little Israel had no prestige and Persian was the great dominating power."[4] This, in turn, appreciatively recalls the saying: "When I am weak, I am strong."

The angels give an impression of working overtime when the time nears for the Savior's birth. One of their number, who identifies himself as *Gabriel*, appeared to Zechariah so as to encourage him that his prayer was heard, and that his wife would bear a child—who would minister in the spirit and power of Elijah (cf. Luke 1:17).

Then, too, Gabriel appeared to Mary—informing her that she would give birth to one who would perpetuate the dynasty of David. Having confided in her, the angel abruptly took his leave. Incidently, there is considerable mention of Gabriel in the extra-biblical writings, where he is represented as one of four chief angels—along with Michael, Raphael, and Uriel.[5] Gabriel, in particular, is portrayed in an intercessory role.

As previously noted, there were shepherds tending their flocks by night, when an angel announced the Savior's birth. Whereupon, he was joined by a host of angels, praising God and saying: "Glory to God in the highest, and on earth peace to men on whom his favor rests" (Luke 2:14). This constituted glad tidings, soliciting great joy.

We hear nothing more concerning angels until one "from heaven appeared to him (Jesus) and strengthened him" (Luke 22:43). "Whether Jesus required angelic assistance is not clarified within the narrative. What is clear is that the presence of the angel empowers Jesus to engage in even more ardent prayer. God's response to Jesus' prayer is to provide strength for the (impending) ordeal."[6]

Then when women arrived at Jesus' tomb to anoint his body for burial, they encountered "two men in clothes that gleamed like lightning"—who announced that Jesus was risen from the dead (Luke 24:4-6). The allusion would appear to be to angels. As such, they are again cast in the role of mentors.

Angels continue to make an appearance from time to time. As an example, the apostles were apprehended, and put in prison. "But during the night an angel of the Lord opened the doors of the jail and brought them out. 'Go, stand in the temple courts,' he said, 'and tell the people the full message of this new life'" (Acts 5:19-20). Details are lacking, leading to pointless speculation. As with Jesus in Gethsemane, the apostles are encouraged to press on in their appointed task.

Subsequently, a great persecution broke out into the surrounding regions, scattering those who were abiding in Jerusalem. In that connection, an angel of the Lord enjoined Philip: "Go south to the road—the desert road—that goes down from Jerusalem to Gaza" (Acts 8:26). There he encountered an Ethiopian eunuch, who was searching the scriptures. Upon sharing the gospel with him, the eunuch believed and was baptized.

There was a God-fearing centurion named *Cornelius*, who was earnestly engaged in prayer when he distinctly saw an angel of God—who admonished him to send a delegation to Peter (cf. Acts 10:4-5). The apostle, in turn, had a vision preparing him for the encounter and subsequent ministry.

Peter was again imprisoned. "Suddenly an angel of the Lord appeared and a light shone in the cell" (Acts 12:7). The apostle was awakened, his chains fell off, and he was instructed to dress. "They passed the first and second guards and came to the iron gate leading to the city. It opened for them by itself, and they went through it. When they had walked the length of the street, suddenly the angel left him." "The narrative bears witness to the delivering grace of God and to the power of believing prayer. That James should die while Peter should escape is a mystery of divine providence which has been repeated countless times in the history of the people of God."[7]

When it dawned on Peter what had happened, he made his way to the house of Mary, the mother of John—also called *Mark*. Those present could not bring themselves to believe that the apostle had escaped, but attributed his appearance to a guardian angel (cf. Acts. 12:15). It was apparently assumed that persons had such to watch out for their welfare.

Conversely, Herod appeared in his royal splendor, to deliver a public address. At which, the populace shouted: "This is the voice of a god not of a man" (Acts 12:22). "Immediately, because (he) did not give praise to God, an angel of the Lord struck him down." Josephus graphically extrapolates: "But, as he afterwards looked up, he saw an owl sitting on a certain rope over his head, and immediately understood that this bird was the messenger of ill tidings . . . and fell into the deepest sorrow."[8] All things considered, it would appear that the angels are bent on comforting the afflicted, and afflicting the objectionably comfortable.

The existence of angels was a matter of dispute. "The Sadducees say that there is no resurrection, and that there are neither angels nor spirits, but the Pharisees acknowledge them all" (Acts 23:8). Paul concurred with the latter.

Luke cites a final instance concerning angels. Paul had set out for Rome when a violent storm threatened to demolish the ship, and terminate all on board. At which an angel appeared to the apostle, saying: "Do not be afraid, Paul. You must stand trial before Caesar, and God has graciously given you the lives of all who sail with you" (Acts 27:24). With this in mind, he encouraged those with him.

In conclusion, we turn to the curious way in which the messages to the seven churches of Revelation are addressed. Expressly, "to the angel of the church in"—followed by the designation (cf. Rev. 2:1, 8, 12, 18; 3:1, 7, 14). Since the several messages are obviously directed to the respective congregations, it would seem that the angels are charged with bringing this to their attention. In any case, it serves to enhance the angelic mystery.

6

HUMAN MYSTERY

"When I consider your heavens, the work of your fingers, the moon and the stars, which you have set in place," the psalmist muses, "what is man that you are mindful of him, the son of man that you care for him? You made him a little lower than the heavenly beings and crowned him with glory and honor" (8:3-5). Consequently, we imagine a pitch black night, offset only by the light of the moon and stars overhead. We seem small and insignificant by comparison.

Yet, we sense within an inhibited preeminence. "You made him ruler over the works of your hands," the psalmist continues; "you put everything under his feet: all flocks and herds, and the beasts of the field, the birds of the air, and the fish of the seas, all that swim the paths of the seas."

A THEOLOGICAL PERSPECTIVE

Defining humans by way of their dominion is a helpful exercise, which James Mays explores in several connections. Initially, "*The administration* of the Lord's reign in the world extends (to all). It can be carried out only in identity with the whole and ultimately fulfilled only by the entire species."[1]

Conversely, the failure on the part of one impacts adversely on the rest. As when one irresponsibly throws trash by the side of the road, or pollutes a stream with garbage. Such behavior makes humanity appear as a cosmic contagion.

Secondly, human dominion extends over both domestic and wild life. As for the former, all that accommodates to human social behavior. As for the latter, that which attempts to manage on its own.

This assumes that humanity will bring its creative genius to bear on forging a better life for the proliferation of life forms. In this regard, man is capable of recalling the past, anticipating the future, and wisely choosing among available options. While one is calculated to make mistakes in the process, he or she should learn thereby.

Thirdly, "the dominion of the human corresponds to and is subordinate to the reign of the creator. Human beings are to use their power over creatures in a way that serves the purposes and practices of their own sovereign."[2] That is to say, in a way in which they would want to be treated.

Accordingly, the legitimacy of their reign draws from its correspondence to God's gracious purposes. In this regard, man will be held strictly accountable. Even now, he either benefits from a faithful stewardship, or suffers for its lack.

Fourthly, the text does not discuss how well man is managing. In contrast, the patriarchal narratives depict humankind as fostering a few suitable individuals, among a vast multitude of those largely indifferent to their calling.

As a result, humanity suffers. Dominion becomes domination, rule becomes ruin, and service becomes self-seeking. As an extended spin-off, the larger creation also suffers. In this regard, "We know that the whole creation has been groaning as in the pains of childbirth right up to the present time" (Rom. 8:22).

Lastly, "It is by the reign of God in and through Christ that all things will be finally made subject to the sovereignty of God. So Christians, as they praise the Lord with this psalm, will do so in penitence and hope, remembering that 'the creation waits with eager longing for the revealing of the children of God' (Rom. 8:19)."[3]

Even now, the Messianic Age has dawned. Consequently, persons can experience an earnest of the future. Will matters get better or worse? Likely both, as the consummation draws near. All things considered, we can earnestly conclude with the psalmist: "O Lord, our Lord, how majestic is your name in all the earth."

A PERSONAL PERSPECTIVE

Of course, the theological perspective is only one among others. One's personal awareness serves as a prime example. While we might be described in various ways, we are single entities. In this regard, one might observe that *my* leg was injured, or *my* feelings hurt.

As such, man is a sensate creature. In the still of the night he feels the cool wisp of air against his flesh, after the sweltering heat of the day. He hears some creature in the nearby brush, and strains to identify it. The faint aroma of wild flowers is hardly perceptible. All these are deftly assimilated and monitored.

This requires no calculated effort, although one can focus on some aspect or another. Whether briefly or for an extended period of time, man establishes priorities. These may be kept to oneself, or shared with others.

Man is also a rational creature. Given the vast extent of the universe and man's minuscule appearance, why should the Almighty be especially concerned for him? Unless, of course, there are extenuating circumstances.

Such proves to be the case. He was created a little lower than the angels, but given rule over God's extended creation. To those to whom much is given, the more is required. Then, too, God endows his creatures with what is needed to fulfill their responsibilities. As a result, man is without excuse for his failures.

Implied in the above line of reasoning, man is likewise a volitional creature. He is not simply passive, but takes initiatives. One can imagine the psalmist shifting his position to get a better perspective on the vast reaches of the nocturnal sky overhead. Then pausing to converse with one of his associates.

Having weighed the implications of living in God's world, he may choose to act upon or neglect them. This gives rise to the distinction between sins of omission and commission. It also accounts for John Calvin's suggestion that one who fails to preserve a life is as one who takes a life.

While sin has both personal and social implications, it is essentially religious in character. Accordingly, "Against you, you only, have I sinned and done what is evil in your sight" (Psa. 51:4). In context, it is not the severity of God's judgment that should concern us, but its uncompromising standard.

Finally, the psalmist exhibits feelings. These are of three sorts. First, there are sentient feelings—associated with his sensate experiences. If concerning the approach of a threatening creature, then fear. If the assurance of needed rain, then with appreciation.

Second, there are feelings related to intuition. Such as when we sense that someone is displeased with our behavior. Or when we are impressed with a divine presence, even when we may attempt to dismiss it.

Finally, there are emotions that accompany our rational process. "The Lord sustains the humble," the psalmist observes, "and casts the wicked to the ground" (147:6). So that one feels encouraged to cultivate the way of righteousness, and restrain from the temptation to go astray.

"Come now, let us reason together," God admonishes, "though your sins are like scarlet, they shall be as white as snow" (Isa. 1:18). "**Reason together** is rather mild, 'argue it out' (NRSV) reminds us that all this takes place in the context of a metaphorical court case between Yahweh and Judah."[4] As a result, it is meant to solicit our deferential attention.

A SOCIAL PERSPECTIVE

"Life originates from an intimate social relationship. I would not persist were it not for the caring concern of others. Except on exceedingly rare occasions, it continues to be nurtured in a supportive social context."[5] Man is inherently a social creature.

"A woman giving birth to a child has pain because her time has come," Jesus empathetically observed, "but when her baby is born she forgets the anguish because of her joy that a child is born into the world" (John 16:21). In a larger context, we are encouraged to believe that painful experiences can cultivate a greater good.

The birthed child is "exposed to a strange and threatening environment. As noted above, it would not long survive without assistance. Its mother is as a rule the primary care-giver. Breast-feeding provides an intimate and satisfactory means."[6]

The infant appears scarcely aware of what is going on around it. Ill-defined images come and go. Sounds rumble in the background. One thing is certain, it is not alone.

It becomes increasingly aware of the parameters of the self. What is mine, as over against what belongs to another or must be shared. *My* toe, although it has not learned the nomenclature. *Your* hand, since it is manipulated by someone else.

It soon learns that crying is an effective means of gaining attention. It cannot as yet articulate its wants, so that another must appraise the situation. While the system leaves much to be desired, it will have to serve for the time being.

The infant becomes more perceptive as time goes on. It can differentiate between its parents. If there are siblings, they too must be singled out. There are additional persons who play a significant role, along with less influential persons.

Social patterns impact on life throughout the maturing process. "Look!" the elder brother protested. "All these years I've been slaving for you and never disobeyed your orders. Yet you never gave me even a young goat so I could celebrate with my friends. But when this son of yours who has squandered your property with prostitutes comes home, you kill the fattened calf for him!" (Luke 15:29-30).

"My son," his father replied, "you are always with me, and everything I have is yours. But we had to celebrate and be glad, because this brother of yours was dead and is alive again; he was lost and is found."

These three perspectives (the theological, personal, and social) bond together in some creative manner to endow life with meaning. In a way common to all, but yet quite distinctive. So that there are no genuine duplicates, not even among identical twins.

BIOGRAPHICAL NOTES

While the psalter is credited to a number of contributors, its prime focus is upon David. This, in turn, encourages us to reflect back upon his experience as a means of sharpening our focus on the mystery that besets humans.

David was the youngest son of Jesse, of the prominent tribe of Judah. His family lived in Bethlehem, six miles south of Jerusalem. Ruth was his great-grandmother. While we know little of his early life, he did take care of his father's sheep. When attacked by wild beasts, he courageously protected the flock. Moreover, he credited God for enabling him to do so (cf. 1 Sam. 17:37).

David was also an accomplished musician. He was solicited in this connection to play for King Saul. While this would seem a rare privilege, it did not seem to significantly alter the way he was perceived in the family—as the youngest son.

Once, when the Israelites were encamped over against their traditional enemies—the Philistines, David was recruited to take supplies to his older brothers.

"On this occasion the Philistines had commandeered a huge Hittite to act as champion, one who would fight on behalf of their army. If an equivalent champion from among the Israelites could defeat him, then the Philistine army agreed to surrender,"[7]

The Israelites were loath to take up the challenge, because of the imposing appearance of their adversary. David, however, offered to accept it, since he believed God would enable him to be the victor. He was correct in his assessment.

When the Israelite forces were returning from their deployment, women heartily greeted them with the lyrics: "Saul has slain his thousands, and David his tens of thousands" (1 Sam. 18:7).This greatly displeased Saul, who from that time on harbored jealously toward the youth. On one occasion, he hurled a spear at him.

David now assumed the role of a hunted fugitive. While taking refuge at Engedi, he could have taken the king's life, but refused to do so—since he was the Lord's anointed. When David heard of the death of Saul and Jonathan, he returned to Hebron—where he was anointed to reign over Judah. Subsequently, he was exalted to king over all of Israel at Jerusalem. In this capacity, he was described as "a man after his (God's) own heart" (1 Sam. 13:14). He continued to be remembered in this regard, as a bench-mark of subsequent rulers. For instance, "As Solomon grew old, his wives turned his heart after other gods, and his heart was not fully devoted to the Lord his God, as the heart of David his father had been" (1 Kings 11:4).

Even so, David's career concluded with a series of personal tragedies. Most notable was that associated with the death of Uriah, the Hittite. One evening David got up from his bed, and walked around on the roof of the palace. From there he could see Bathsheba, the wife of Uriah, bathing. She was very beautiful, and he sent for her. When she conceived, he summoned Uriah—who was deployed in battle, and encouraged him to return home to his wife. When he refused, the king plotted to have him killed in battle. He thus compounded the sin of adultary with murder.

Subsequently, Nathan the prophet confronted David with his trespasses. David contritely replied, "I have sinned against the Lord" (1 Sam. 12:13). In keeping with its ascription, Psalm 51 recalls this dramatic encounter. "Have mercy on me, O God, according to your great compassion blot out my transgressions" (v. 1). "David did not mince words. He did not admit to making a mistake, but having sinned. He did not ask for a definition of sin, but stated the obvious. He did not attempt to hide from himself what he admitted to others."[8] We will allow the psalmist the final word: "I praise you because I am fearfully and wonderfully made" (139:14).

7

UNIVERSAL MYSTERY

Although the origin of the universe is obscure, "These days most cosmologists and astronomers back the theory that there was indeed a creation, about eighteen billion years ago, when the physical universe burst into existence in an awesome explosion popularly known as the 'big bang."[1] "The earth, for example, cannot have existed for ever, or its core would have cooled down. From radioactivity studies the Earth can be dated to about 4 ½ billion years, which is similar to the age of the moon and of various meteorites."[2]

In greater detail, "We live on one small planet, circling an ordinary star in just one of 100 billion stars in the Milky Way galaxy. Our galaxy is one among many millions in the Universe."[3] It is deemed necessary for something of the sort to occur for life to have evolved and been sustained.

In any case, "The origin of life remains one of the great scientific mysteries. This central conundrum is the threshold problem. Only when organic molecules achieve a certain very high level of complexity can they be considered as 'living.'"[4] In addition, it is a highly unlikely scenario; soliciting the observation that were life to disappear, we can be reasonably assured that it would not return.

The Genesis account is said to convey how things would have appeared from an observer's perspective. It goes without saying that its language lacks scientific precision or that the primary focus is on the Almighty and his instrumental role in bringing the universe into existence. As succinctly expressed, "In the beginning God created the heavens and the earth" (Gen. 1:1). *In the beginning* likely corresponds to *the time of the gods* in traditional literature. As such, it concerns a time before man came on the scene, and the gods jostled around for position. Conversely, the creation account portrays God in his singular splendor.

Traditional people would readily identify the reference to *God* as the *High God*. "In fact, belief in the High God appears so pervasive among traditional peoples as to be virtually without exception. It is said that he is called by several thousand

names on record. Some have supposed this (reflective) of an original monotheism."[5]
By way of confirmation, I was solemnly assured by a village person: "Although we
have different names for him, he is one and the same."

Wilhelm Schmidt attributed six characteristics to the High God: eternity, omniscience, beneficence, morality, omnipotence, and creative power. For instance, he
observes: "A sort of *eternity* is ascribed to all these Supreme Beings more or less
clearly, whenever we have anything like detailed information. The form of the
statements is that they existed before all other beings, have always been and always
will be, or that they never die."[6]

Worthy of note, God is set forth as *the sufficient cause* for bringing into
existence the heavens and the earth, a comprehensive idiom for the universe in its
entirety. This, in turn, recalls a humorous interchange between God and a
disgruntled individual. "I could have created a better universe," the latter
complained.

"Go ahead," the Almighty heartily encouraged him.

At this, he stooped down to pick up some dirt. "Get your own dirt," God protested. His effort was thereby aborted.

Of course, the Genesis narrative implies that the God who created the universe
is also actively engaged in maintaining it—in keeping with his benevolent purposes.
This, moreover, means to solicit our appreciative cooperation. Whereas a failure to
do so invites a disaster of major proportions.

"The idea of space being created out of nothing is a subtle one that many people
find hard to understand, especially if they are used to thinking of space as already
being 'nothing,'" Paul Davies allows. "The physicist, however, regards space as
more like an elastic medium. To the physicist 'nothing' means 'no space' as well
as no matter."[7] Then, too, creation marks the beginning of time as we know it. Consequently, we live within a space/time continuum.

"Now the earth was formless and empty, darkness was over the surface of the
deep, and the Spirit of God was hovering over the waters." "This combination of
terms occurs only here and with reference to the disintegration of the social order
following the Babylonian invasion (cf. Jer. 32:1). . . . While not inviting, chaos
appears as the first step in the creative process."[8] Only later does it take on pronounced negative connotations, as if resulting from a rejection of the divinely appointed order.

In any case, a brief running commentary would seem eminently in order. "Let
there be light," God initially enjoins, and there was light. God saw that the light was
good, and he separated the light from the darkness." He called the light *day*, and the
darkness *night*. "And there was evening, and there was morning—the first day."
Whether in this connection or some other, there is a logical progression running
throughout the extended account of creation.

The refrain *And God said* is repeated six times in all. This is by way of
emphasis. It also serves to impress on the reader his sovereign prerogative in
particularizing the various aspects of creation.

The term *yom* can be used in conjunction with a solar day of twenty-four hours, the daylight portion thereof, or in a figurative sense concerning an indeterminate period of time. If a solar day was meant, then the successive days need not be consecutive. Incidently, a solar day may be differentiated as to dawn (cf. Job 3:9), noon (cf. 1 Sam. 11:11), cool of the day—late afternoon (cf. Gen. 3:8), and evening (cf. Ruth 2:17).

If employed in a figurative sense, the designation is often characterized by its defining feature—as with *the day of the Lord*. In this instance, the allusion would be to the days of creation. There was evening and morning, constituting the first day. It is for this reason that Jewish tradition reckons the day from sundown to sundown.

"And God said, 'Let there be an expanse between the waters, to separate the water from water.' . . . And it was so." God called the expanse *sky*, and that set apart the second day. One could readily imagine the enveloping vapors retreating from the ocean surface in this connection.

The *Enuma Elish* provides a strikingly fanciful contrast to the empirical oriented Genesis text:

Then the Lord (Marduk) rested, examined her dead body (Tiamat).
To divide the abortion and create ingenious things therewith.
To split her open like a mussel in two parts;
Half of her he set in place and formed the sky therewith as a roof.

"And God said, 'Let the water under the sky be gathered to one place, and let dry ground appear.' And it was so." God called the dry ground *land*, and the gathered waters he called *seas*. And God saw that it was *good*, which is to say that it was functional and aesthetically pleasing.

"Then God said, 'Let the land produce vegetation: seed-bearing plants and trees on the land that bear fruit with seed in it, according to their various kinds.' And it was so." God saw that it was good, and so concludes the third day. An ecosystem was obviously in the making. Jewish tradition would recall this feature as a mandate to function within God-given parameters.

"And God said, 'Let there be lights in the expanse of the sky to separate the day from the night, and let them serve as signs to mark seasons and days and years, and let them be lights in the expanse of the sky to give light on the earth.' And it was so." He made the greater light to rule over the day, and the lesser light to reign over the night. God also set the stars in the heavens. He saw that it was good, and so the fourth day came to an appreciative conclusion.

As an aside, this made it possible to construct a liturgical calendar. Then, in turn, it provided a means to cultivate the sacred character of life. As noted in an earlier context, so as to live under a sacred canopy. In this manner, to honor God in all we say and do.

And God said, "Let the water teem with living creatures, and let birds fly above the earth across the expanse of the sky." "So God created the great creatures of the sea and every living and moving thing with which the water teems, according to their kinds, and every winged bird according to its kind." Having determined that this was good, the Almighty blessed them, saying: "Be fruitful and increase in number and fill the water in the seas, and let the birds increase on the earth." All this took place on the fifth day.

The rabbis reasoned that God refrained from blessing the flora, since it would respond naturally to the sun and rain. Conversely, volition played a rule with the fauna. Theophilus elaborated in this regard: "For as the fish and fowls . . . some indeed abide in their natural state, and do no harm to those weaker than themselves, but keep the law of God . . . ; others of them, again, transgress the law of God, and eat flesh, and injure those weaker than themselves."[9]

"And God said, 'Let the land produce living creatures according to their kinds: livestock, creatures that move along the ground, and wild animals, each according to its kind.' And it was so." After that, God saw that it was good.

"Then God said, 'Let us make man in our image, in our likeness, and let them rule over the fish of the sea and the birds of the air, over the livestock, over all the earth, and over all the creatures that move along the ground.'" So God created man in his image, male and female he created them—so that they comprised corporate man. As previously expressed, the expression *let us* appears to be a royal idiom—not unlike its subsequent usage, when the pontiff employs a plural form.

Furthermore, he blessed and commanded them: "Be fruitful and increase in number; fill the earth and subdue it. Rule over the fish of the sea and the birds of the air and over every living creature that moves on the ground." The repetition is by way of emphasis, meant to underscore man's delegated responsibility. Thereafter, God surveyed all that he had made, and concluded that it was exceedingly good. Each in its own right, as previously mentioned, but especially as a composite.

The decision to make mankind in God's image served as climax to his creative activity. As such, it resembled a capstone, intended to hold the structure in place. Without which it was calculated to fall into disarray.

The *imago dei* can be viewed from three complimentary perspectives. Initially, we are alerted to the fact that it was God's intent that man should commune with him. While this constitutes a special privilege, it should be remembered that to whom much is given, more is required.

Communion is contingent on compatibility. Accordingly, the prophet rhetorically inquires: "Do two walk together unless they have agreed to do so?" (Amos 3:2). Assuredly not! Consequently, it is for man to adjust in order to accommodate the Almighty and his righteous ways.

Secondly, man is enjoined to embrace his role as steward of God's extended creation. More precisely, he is to serve on the Lord's behalf, at his bequest, and as accountable to him. In so doing, he implements God's purposeful design, rather than allowing it to slip back into chaotic turmoil.

As elucidated by the rabbis, this required that he first put his own house in order. Should he fail to resist the evil inclination within, he would be incapable of dealing with the threat from without. As popularly expressed, man proves to be his own worst enemy. This was graphically illustrated during the turbulent time of the judges, when persons were disposed to do whatever seemed appealing to them.

Finally, man was uniquely qualified for his rigorous calling. This can be illustrated from his aptness in the use of language. By this means, he could recall the past, anticipate the future, and choose among the available alternatives.

This, moreover, brings to mind one of my favorite quotes—attributed to Mother Theresa. "I have no doubt but that God gives me the means to accomplish what he calls me to do," she mused. "However, I wished he were not so optimistic."

The Lord formed man from the dust of the ground, and breathed into his nostrils the breath of life. He was thus animated. While he might be described in various ways, he was essentially a composite creature. This was unlike the Greek version, which portrayed him as a soul imprisoned in a body.

This recalls the striking dissimilarity between the deaths of Socrates and Jesus. As for the former, he welcomed execution as a release from his bodily confinement. As for the latter, Jesus preferred not to encounter the ordeal, but deferred to his Father's will in the matter. "Where, O death, is your victory?" Paul subsequently inquired. "Where, O death, is your sting" (1 Cor. 15:55). Then, by way of clarification: "The sting of death is sin, and the power of sin is the law. But thanks be to God! He gives us the victory through our Lord Jesus Christ!" Emphatically so!

God rested on the seventh day from all his creative activity, and hallowed it as a special time for worship. As a result, Jewish tradition distinguished between labor thought analogous to God's creative activity—such as igniting a fire, and other forms of endeavor.

In addition, the rabbis reasoned that unless man was industrious throughout the week, he would be incapable of properly observing the Sabbath. In this regard, he was enjoined to take care of his own needs, and the needs of others. Especially was he obligated to assist those unable to manage their own needs.

On the one hand, we are not altogether able to appreciate God's continued presence, since we have never experienced anything apart from it. On the other, we have difficulty imagining what man would be apart from his fallen condition, and its adverse impact on creation at large. So it is that the universal mystery runs its course.

8

PROPHECY

To *prophesy* is to declare. While it may involve future events, they are not necessary. Even when incorporated, prophecy has application for the present. Also worthy of note, we are less driven by the past than drawn by the future.

In this regard, the Christian faith revolves around a personal deity. As such, his transcendence is implicit. Consequently, he can only be known as he chooses to reveal himself. The stage is thus set for a discussion of the prophetic mystery.

In greater detail, the human analogy is apt. We can gain some impression of a person by the way he acts. Wisdom literature serves to remind us of this when it comes to the Almighty. Even so, some persons are more alert than others.

Prophetic literature carries self-disclosure to another level. This as a rule follows the pattern of events, which solicit divine commentary. It, moreover, accounts for the prophetic signature *thus God says*.

Apocalyptic literature rounds out the short list of literary genre. Common discourse fails us in this instance, so that we have to rely on graphic imagery. We are left with lingering impressions impossible of more explicit interpretation.

Were this not sufficiently confusing, genre blend together in select ways to suit the author's intent. Accordingly, while the Revelation is often characterized as apocalyptic, it provides a creative mix of literary genre.

Wisdom literature first invites our attention. When the term *wisdom* is not interchangeable with *knowledge*, it characteristically touches on application. I was reminded of this some years ago while having lunch in the college cafeteria with clinical psychologist Donald Tweedie. A student paused at our table to solicit his advice concerning the selection of a major.

Noted for his unpredictable and thought-provoking observations, the astute counselor observed: "It probably doesn't matter all that much what major you select. Pick out an instructor who has insight into life, and learn all you can from him or her." In other words, opt for a person skilled in living.

Consider some of the cast in wisdom literature. It goes without saying, there is the *sage* person. He or she welcomes instruction, by way of obtaining understanding. With insight, cultivates skill in living; with skill, able to plan ahead; with all, equipped to orient life toward God and his righteous will. In this connection, "Blessed is the man (whose) delight is in the law of the Lord, and on his law he meditates day and night" (Psa. 1:1-2). He resembles a tree planted by the bank of a stream, that brings forth fruit in season, and maintains its vigor throughout the seasons.

The *fool* provides a study in contrasts. He is inattentive to instruction, and content with the status quo. As sometimes expressed, he "resembles an accident waiting to happen." Accordingly, he is a menace to himself and to others.

The *scoffer* is a kindred soul. Not only does he despise instruction, but holds it up to ridicule. As such, he is a candidate for Jesus' rebuke: "Why do you look at the speck of sawdust in your brother's eye and pay no attention to the plank in your own eye?" (Matt. 7:3).

The *sluggard* is less militant. He is simply disinclined to undertake worthwhile activity. Otherwise, he is indisposed to carry it through to a successful conclusion. Nor is he inclined to face up to issues, preferring to withdraw from uncomfortable situations. As a result, he often appears restless, helpless, useless, and/or exasperating.

Along more favorable lines, *friendship* is eminently worth cultivating. "A friend loves at all times, and a brother is born for adversity" (Prov. 17:17). As popularly expressed, "A friend in need is a friend indeed."

Finally, the *simple person* is in need of instruction. He should be considered a likely candidate unless disproved. Initial impressions can be misleading, so that a timely approach may be necessary.

All things considered, "The fear of the Lord is the beginning of knowledge" (Prov. 1:7). "*The beginning* (i.e., the first and controlling principle, rather than a state which one leaves behind, cf. Eccles. 12:13) is not merely a right method of thought but a right relation; a worshiping submission (*fear*) to the God of the covenant."[1] All else hinges on cultivating a wholesome relationship with the Almighty.

Given this premise, practical applications fall into place. "Go to the ant, you sluggard, consider its ways and be wise!" (Prov. 6:6). I have been there, and done that—as a child intent on watching the ants scurry around, busily engaged in their activity. Whether this served to enhance my industry is hard to say.

As noted in passing, prophetic literature introduces a more explicit form of revelation. The text of Amos serves to confirm this thesis. Initially, "The words of Amos, one of the shepherds of Tekoa—what he saw concerning Israel two years before the earthquake, when Uzziah was king of Judah and Jeroboam son of Jehoash was king of Israel" (Amos 1:1). Hence, the words are no less his own for being divinely inspired, even though he may appear an unlikely candidate, since he was not associated with the school of the prophets, but rather a shepherd.

He also identifies the occasion for his prophesy. This provides a ready means by which to interpret the text. While applicable to other situations, one must approach the task with the greatest of care. As graphically expressed, it involves the fusion of two horizons—that of the original text and the subsequent situation.

"This is what the Lord says," the prophet confidently declares—concerning Israel and its neighbors. This is by way of confirming the observation: "Righteousness exalts a nation, but sin is a disgrace to any people" (Prov. 14:34). Then, too, God allows for no exceptions.

Upon closer scrutiny, one can readily distinguish a variety of literary forms. "*Judgment speeches* (constitute) the backbone of the book. They may be introduced by a 'messenger formula', usually include an accusation (or indictment) of sin and an announcement (or threat) of punishment . . . and may conclude with an oracle."[2]

Vision reports comprise a second major component of the text (cf. 7:1-3, 4-6, 7-9; 8:1-2, 9:1-4). A more extensive list of literary forms would include biographical narrative (7:10-17), the promise of deliverance (9:11-15), repetition (3:3-6), call to attention (3:1; 4:1), quotations (2:12; 4:1), response to voiced opposition (2:11; 3:3-8), punning (55:5; 8:1-2), and gestures (4:12).

Amos sets out to address the degenerate political, social, and religious life of the northern kingdom. "Formal recognition of the implications of the Mosaic Covenant was not sufficient to restore the vitality of Israelite national life. Instead, the spiritual essence of the Covenant had to become the dominating concern of all, lest divine retribution overtake them for their wickedness."[3]

The message is played out against the backdrop of the anticipated Day of the Lord. Should any fail to respond, it will come as a time of judgment rather than vindication, darkness instead of light. Consequently, one could not afford to procrastinate.

"I hate, I despise your religious feasts; I cannot stand your assemblies," the Lord protests (5:21. "But let justice roll on like a river, righteousness like a neverfailing stream!" The imagery is drawn from river beds, dry most of the year, but gushing water during the rainy season. It intends to urge the people to be zealous and constant in their pursuit of justice in conformity to God's righteous ways.

Two oracles comprise the conclusion to the text (9:11-15). Both focus on the prospect of restoration. For instance, "In that day I will restore David's fallen tent. I will repair its broken places, restore its ruins, and build it as it used to be, so that they may possess the remnant of Edom, and all the nations that bear my name."

God remains faithful even when man proves faithless. Beyond despair, there remains a resilient hope. In classic terms: "When I shut up the heavens, command locusts to devour the land, or send a plague among my people, if (they) will humble themselves, seek my face, and turn from their wicked ways, then will I hear from heaven and will forgive their sins and will heal their land" (2 Chron. 7:13-14).

Two related questions readily come to mind. First, what manner of deity is this that opts to reveal his truths to wayward creatures? "Give thanks to the Lord for he is good," the psalmist enthuses; "his love endures forever" (107:1). This introduces a praise text concerning the loyal love of the Lord shown in marvelous works of deliverance performed in answer to the cry of those in distress. The celebrants, in turn, are identified as all whom the Lord has redeemed from adversity and gathered from around the world.

He will not compromise his righteousness, nor will he withdraw his compassion. This translates into a probationary period, either seized upon or squandered. As C. S. Lewis reminds us, only God knows when more time will serve no constructive purpose.

Second, what manner of person does God employ to convey his message? While Abraham Heschel explores this topic in depth, two excerpts will suffice to suggest his line of reasoning. "The prophet is human, yet he employs notes one octave too high for our ears. He experiences moments that defy our understanding. . . . Often his words begin to burn as our conscience ends."[4] To mix metaphors, he resolutely marches to a different cadence.

Then, too, the prophetic utterances reveal a profound empathy with God's disposition, in contrast to the relative disregard of the general populace. As when he laments over human degradation, or conversely his rejoicing with the reclamation of a lost soul.

Apocalyptic literature next awaits our attention. The genre reveals three prime characteristics. "In the first place, it is *eschatological*. It treats a time yet future when God will break into the world of time and space to bring the entire system to a final reckoning."[5] While the prophets customarily alluded to the future out of deference to the present, the apocalyptic writer anticipated the future that would break into the present.

We are thus alerted to the limits of our understanding concerning what will unfold in the future. Prophecy, to touch back on the previous topic, should not be portrayed simply as history written beforehand. I was reminded of this one day when watching a man astride a donkey, riding into Jerusalem. I did not seriously consider that he might be the Messiah.

In addition, apocalyptic literature is *dualistic*. There are two opposing supernatural powers, God and Satan. "There are also two distinct ages: the present one that is temporal and evil, and the one to come that is timeless and perfectly righteous. Closely related . . . is the idea of two worlds, the present visible universe and the perfect world that has existed from before time in heaven."[6]

By way of illustration, John writes: "After this I looked, and there before me was a door standing open to heaven And the voice I had first heard speaking to me like a trumpet said, 'Come up here, and I will show you what must take place after this'" (Rev. 4:1). In that instance, his attention is drawn away from the seven churches to consider what is transpiring behind the scene.

Finally, apocalyptic literature portrays life as moving "forward as divinely preordained according to a definite time schedule and toward a predetermined end." This, in turn, "bred confidence that God would emerge victorious."[7] It also served to put suffering in the light of God's redemptive purpose.

Worthy of note in this connection, God is not inhibited by the constraint of time—as are we. Tomorrow is as lucid to him as today. As a result, his promises remain trustworthy—in spite of every adverse consideration.

These characteristics assert themselves through the literary features of apocalyptic discourse. The content of apocalypse often comes to the author by means of a dream or vision, in which he is translated into heavenly realms—there to reflect on God's resolute intent. An angelic guide not uncommonly makes an appearance to acquaint him with unfamiliar surroundings, where he confronts strange creatures—representing the forces of good and evil.

One illustration will suffice. "A great and wondrous sign appeared in heaven," John records: "a woman clothed with the sun, with the moon under her feet and a crown of twelve stars on her head. She was pregnant and cried out in pain as she was about to give birth" (Rev. 12:1-2).

"Then another sign appeared in heaven: an enormous red dragon with seven heads, and ten horns and seven crowns on his heads. His tail swept a third of the stars out of the sky and flung them to the earth." It stood in front of the woman, to devour the child she would birth.

When a male child was born, it was snatched up to heaven. Whereupon, the woman fled to the desert, to a sanctuary prepared by God for her. Then there was war in heaven, between Michael and his angels against the dragon and its angelic subordinates. Here the dragon is identified as "that ancient serpent, called the devil or Satan, who leads the whole world astray."

When the dragon saw that the battle was lost, he pursued the woman who had given birth, but she was given the wings of a great eagle to make good her escape. Then the dragon made war against the rest of her offspring: "Those who obey God's commandments and hold to the testimony of Jesus." While the narrative continues, we take our leave at this juncture—quite convinced of the mysterious component in divine revelation.

9

THE AFTERLIFE

The previous topic leads quite naturally into the present one—concerning the afterlife. We view its prospect from the middle, between paradise lost and regained. Accordingly, our perspective is inhibited. Still, it is not something to be ignored nor minimized.

"There are, aren't there, only three things we can do about death: to desire it, to fear it, or to ignore it?"[1] As for the first of these options, "Socrates cannot fear death, since indeed it sets us free from the body. Whoever fears death proves that he loves the world of the body, that he is thoroughly entangled in the world of the senses. Death is the soul's great friend."[2] This cogently illustrates the classic Greek concept of the immortality of the soul.

Qualifications aside, Jesus' death may be said to illustrate the second of the three alternatives. "Death for him is not something divine; it is something dreadful. Jesus does not want to be alone in this moment. He knows, of course that the Father stands by to help him. He looks to him in this decisive moment as he had done throughout his life."[3] This is in confident assurance of his resurrection.

Then, finally, there are those who ignore death as best they can. Such as the affluent man D. L. Moody graphically describes. It seems that he proudly pointed out to the evangelist that all he could see from their elevated vantage point belonged to him. In response, Moody pointed toward the expanse above, with the inquiry of how much he had invested in his eternal account.

The death of a loved one is often a memorable event. In a certain instance, it was more memorable than most. When her critical condition became known, the extended family gathered to await her passing. Meanwhile, she slipped into a coma.

Upon regaining consciousness, she asked that the family gather by her bedside. "My trust is in the Lord," she assured them, "and I am anticipating what lies before me." "However," she added, "some of you remain unprepared. This is a concern for me." The woman passed away about a half hour later.

In any case, we go to great lengths to disguise the reality of death. We employ such euphemisms as *falling asleep, expiring,* or *passing away.* The embalmer goes to great length in order to give the impression of life. This, in turn, solicits the observation that he or she *looks so natural.*

"To the existentialist, the unwillingness to come to grips with the reality of death is a prime example of 'inauthentic existence.' Death is one of the harsh realities of life: every individual is going to grow old, die, be taken to the cemetery and buried in the ground."[4] A person who has not come to grips with the prospect of death is not genuinely prepared to live properly.

While most would agree that death occurs, its precise nature is less obvious. It would seem to mark the conclusion of life in its bodily form. Whether life persists in some other manner constitutes a different but related issue. Initially, it would seem strange that life which holds such great potential would come to an abrupt end. Common sense would seem to dictate otherwise.

In addition, belief in a future life is virtually pervasive among traditional peoples. As an example, "In the Chinese mind, it is believed that ancestor spirits live in the 'other world' as much as they (lived) while on earth. Hence they must be fed, cared for and propitiated."[5] The failure to do so may result in the ancestor becoming disgruntled and even malevolent.

The mystery associated with the afterlife can be illustrated in various ways. Accordingly, a certain woman drew me aside to inquire about something she had experienced. It seems that she awoke to a luminous appearance by her bedroom door. "What was it?" she curiously inquired—supposing I might have some theological explanation. When I proposed that it might be the reflection of the headlights of a car, she did not think this likely. When I inquired of her what she thought it might have been, she indicated that it could have been the spirit of her mother.

"Why would she want to be making an appearance?" I skeptically inquired.

"To assure me of the afterlife," she responded.

At this, I shared with her that my confidence was more tangible, being associated with Jesus' resurrection. In this regard, "But Christ has indeed been raised from the dead, the firstfruits of those who have fallen asleep" (1 Cor. 15:20). This refers "to the first sheaf of the harvest, which was brought to the temple and offered to God (cf. Lev. 23:10f); it consecrated the whole harvest. . . . His resurrection was to a life that knows no death, and in that sense he was the first and the forerunner of all those who were to be in him."[6]

"But someone may ask, 'How are the dead raised?'" As succinctly expressed, in a form suitable to the resurrected life. Just as our earthly bodies were suited to our temporal existence. In particular, it will be imperishable. Consequently, he does not think of death as non-existence, but as a transition from one existence to another.

As an aside, there is a difference of opinion as to whether physical death is a natural phenomenon, or a result of man's defection. The latter seems more likely, since physical death provides a stark reminder of his alienation. Conversely, had he not sinned, he presumably would have eaten of the tree of life.

How, then, are we to view death? For the unrepentant, it signals the end of lost opportunity. What could have been, no longer will be. Perhaps best concluded not with a period but an exclamation mark.

Jesus told a story concerning a beggar—named *Lazarus*, and a rich man, which graphically illustrates the point. Now the affluent individual enjoyed all the advantages that accrued to his privileged position, while the poor man had barely enough on which to get by. The former was apparently disinclined to share with the less fortunate.

The time came when the beggar died, and the angels carried him to Abraham's side. The rich man also died, and lifting up his eyes in torment, requested that Lazarus bring relief to him. "Son," Abraham replied, "remember that in your lifetime you received your good things, while Lazarus received bad things, but now he is comforted here and you are in agony" (Luke 16:25). In addition, there is a gulf fixed—so that one cannot pass from one abode to the other.

"Then I beg you," the rich man turned beggar employed, "send Lazarus to my father's house, for I have five brothers. Let him warn them, so that they will not also come to this place of torment."

The patriarch replied, "They have Moses and the Prophets; let them listen to them."

"No, father Abraham," the intercessor protested, "but if someone from the dead goes to them, they will repent."

"If they do not listen to Moses and the Prophets," the patriarch observed, "they will not be convinced even if someone rises from the dead."

We would thus conclude that the prospect of death contrasts for the indulgent rich man, and poverty stricken Lazarus. While for the former, the best was past; for the latter, the best was yet to come. In keeping with these options, one should not procrastinate.

There are various terms employed to describe the future abode of the righteous, *heaven* being the most common. In this context, the term coveys the idea of God's habitation. Heaven's prime incentive is to be in God's presence. This will compensate for anything distinctively associated with temporal existence, and greatly enhance all that remains.

Closely coupled with being in God's presence is the realization of *shalom* (peace, well-being). As I like to characterize it, where the train runs on time—every time. Where everything functions as it should, and everyone is considerate of others. In a situation that seems too good to be true, but is true.

It would also appear that our knowledge would be comprehensive. "For we know in part and we prophesy in part," Paul allows, "but when perfection comes, the imperfect disappears. . . . Now we see but a poor reflection in a mirror, then we shall see face to face. Now I know in part; then I shall know fully, even as I am fully known" (1 Cor. 13:9, 12).

Our present knowledge is incomplete, both intensively and extensively. As for the former, the more we know about something, the more we realize that we do not know. As for the latter, we fail to appreciate how the complex facets of life fit together. Still, the apostle assures us that in heaven we resolve all such temporal limitations.

Heaven will also be characterized by the removal of all evil influences. God "will wipe away every tear from their eyes, and death shall be no more, neither shall there be mourning nor crying nor pain any more, for the former things have passed away" (Rev. 21:4). Not only such afflictions, but the very source of evil itself.

All that will remain is unmitigated good. Good expressed without inhibition, and good without the need for compensation. It will not be restricted to some particular occasion, but serve as an unremitting feature of the heavenly existence.

Likewise, God's glory will be manifest in heaven. There will be no need of sun or moon to illumine the new Jerusalem for "the glory of God is its light, and its lamp is the Lamb" (Rev. 21:23; cf. Isa. 24:23). God's *glory* is associated with his majesty and moral perfection. It is unparalleled although relatively obscured for the time being.

It brings to mind the dawn of a new day, with the sun peaking above the horizon. Meanwhile the darkness recedes—along with all the evil things done under the cover of night. However, in this instance the darkness will not return. Accordingly, heaven may be said to accommodate the *children of light*.

We are told relatively little about the activities of the redeemed in heaven. "One quality of our life in heaven will be rest. The writer of the letter to the Hebrews makes much of this concept. Rest, as the term is used in Hebrews, is not merely a cessation of activities, but the experience of reaching a goal of critical importance."[7] As when one has finished a race.

It would seem that those inhabiting heaven would be busily engaged in glorifying God in *both* word and deed. It seems quite impossible to identify these deeds, except to affirm that they will be as a feature of service, gladly rendered, and appreciatively received.

"In my Father's house are many rooms," Jesus informed his disciples. "I am going there to prepare a place for you. And if I go and prepare a place for you, I will come back and take you to be with me that you also may be where I am" (John 14:2-3). Consequently, heaven amounts to a home-coming.

This, in turn, reminds me of the time I returned home from serving overseas during World War II. As I watched out the train window, I could make out the bridge under which I would paddle my boat when fishing. A short way along, we came to a stretch that ran along a forested area that led up to the crest of a hill behind our family dwelling. We turned the corner, and pulled up to the railway station.

I acknowledged some acquaintances, and headed without further delay to my father's general store. I found him with his back turned to the counter. He turned around just as I bent forward, and a startled expression came across his face. Pausing briefly, I headed across the road where my mother awaited me. A friend had rushed from the station to alert her that I was coming. There were tears of joy, especially since she had an intuition that I would not return safely.

I suppose that the introduction to heaven will somewhat resemble this experience, only much preferred. There will be unbridled joy.

Conversely, hell has little to recommend it. Put in its most favorable light, C. S. Lewis suggests that it is the last place a loving deity provides for those who will accept nothing better from him. In contrast to heaven, it is banishment from God's presence.

Jesus does not leave in doubt whether one should risk eventuating in hell. "And if your right hand causes you to sin," he speculated on one occasion, "cut it off and throw it away. It is better for you to lose one part of your body than for your whole body to go into hell (gehenna)" (Matt. 5:29). While not to be taken literally, it was a forceful way of expressing one's avoidance of evil.

The imagery is derived from the Valley of Hinnom, which runs south of Jerusalem and accommodated the trash that smoldered throughout the day and night. The Institute of Holy Land Studies (renamed Jerusalem University College), which I administered for four years, looked out over *the shoulder of Hinnom*. Now and then toward late afternoon, I would make my way down into the valley—bent on discovering some fragments of broken pottery. It is for this reason, that I have come to associate hell with the repository for that which no longer serves the purpose for which God intended it.

If this were not punishment enough, humans are depicted as left to their own devices—apart from the loving constraint of a benevolent deity. I could imagine as a result a thoroughly ineffective bureaucracy, that increasingly compounds the problems of society. Yes, and tedious campaign rhetoric tied to partisan rancor. If not this, then something worse.

God encourages persons to take the preferable option. According to C. S. Lewis, this more often takes the form of *carrots* (incentives) than *clubs*. I had this in mind when composing *Whispers of Heaven*. One example will suffice: "Taps is played at a military burial. Since it is the last thing a soldier hears at day's end, it seems appropriate to render it at the close of life. As such, it is said to express confidence in the resurrection reveille that follows."[8]

10

THE MIRACULOUS

"Jesus did many other miraculous signs in the presence of his disciples, which are not recorded in this book," John readily admits. "But these are written that you may believe that Jesus is the Christ, the Son of God, and that by believing you may have life in his name" (John 20:30-31). It goes without saying that miracles are extraordinary events. Otherwise, they would not be singled out from routine matters.

More expressly, the purpose of miracles is not simply to confound persons, but as a witness. This does not rule out the possibility that they can fulfill a humanitarian purpose. For instance, as concerns the healing miracles, which also serve along the line of salvation parables.

Contrary to popular opinion, miracles do not strictly speaking constitute a violation of natural order. They more resemble an intrusion. C. S. Lewis illustrates this by a person who deflects the course of a billiard ball, only to have it continue along its altered course until it has lost momentum.

Now, of course, miracles did not originate with Jesus. In fact, "They come on great occasions: they are found at the great ganglions of history—not of political or social history, but the spiritual history which cannot be fully known by men. If your own life does not happen to be near one of these great ganglions, how should you expect to see one?"[1] Such as the deliverance of the Israelites from bondage, the struggle of the prophets with Baalism, the life and ministry of Jesus, and the acts of his apostles.

Of course, miracles may occur without our being aware of them. One reason for this is that we become accustomed to screening out the miraculous, particularly when indoctrinated from a naturalistic perspective. As with the person who insists that miracles do not happen because they cannot.

As for *these great ganglions*, they occur at critical junctures in salvation history. They serve in a similar manner to road signs. Apart from them, we would be uninformed of God's most recent initiatives.

Initially, it bears repeating that Moses was tending his father-in-law's sheep, when he witnessed a burning bush that was not consumed. This struck him as something quite out of the ordinary. "I will go over and see that strange sight," he deliberately concluded, "why the bush does not burn up" (Exod. 3:3).

As he approached the bush, a voice called out to him: "Take off the your sandals, for the place where you are standing is holy ground." Afterward, the voice was identified as *the God of your fathers*. If hard pressed to explain this on some objective grounds, the skeptic can always attribute it to some mental state of mind. Conversely, miracles would seem eminently more plausible if one were living in the midst of one of the before-mentioned ganglions—where they occur with greater frequency.

Now God confided in Moses his concern for the Israelites' suffering in bondage, and his intent to deliver them. The Almighty also notified him that he was to be the instrument of deliverance. He was understandably reticent, but God insisted that a little faith in a great God would accomplish the task.

The scene shifts. Moses and his brother Aaron stood before Pharaoh and enjoined him: "This is what the Lord, the God of Israel says: 'Let my people go, so that they may hold a festival to me in the desert'" (5:1).

"Who is the Lord?" the potentate inquired. "The question may include ignorance of the very name of what pharaoh may have considered as some new god of the desert people. In the main, it expresses incredulity at the sheer audacity of the challenge to his absolute authority."[2] This was guaranteed by the Egyptian pantheon.

However, the latter proved to be no match for the Almighty. A series of plagues followed, one on the heels of another. Some have suggested that these resulted from natural causes, such as flooding during the spring rains and/or the fallout of volcanic activity. Were these contributing factors, one would still be hard put to explain away their timing and magnitude.

The death of the firstborn of the land requires some additional rationale. One unlikely scenario accounts for it by speculating that the firstborn slept on the first floor, where the child was more susceptible to poison gas released by seismic activity. Not only would one assume that others slept on the first floor, but the geological character of the region does not lend itself to this explanation. Of course, sceptics can turn to hyperbole or idiomatic expression as a last resort.

A second ganglion concerns the prophets' struggle with the entrenched worship of Baal. Baal was the god of fertility, which included agriculture, animal husbandry, and human sexuality. It appealed to the Israelites not only as a means to negotiate their new surroundings, but that it accommodated their baser inclinations.

It came to pass that there was a severe drought, indicative of the Lord's displeasure with his recalcitrant people. After some time had transpired, the Lord enjoined Elijah: "Go and present yourself to Ahab, and I will send rain on the land" (1 Kings 18:1). So the prophet set out to do the Lord's bidding.

When Ahab saw Elijah, he inquired: "Is that you, you troubler of Israel?"

"I have not made trouble for Israel," the prophet protested. "But you and your father's family have. You have abandoned the Lord's commands and have followed the Baals. Now summon the people from all over Israel to meet me on Mount

Carmel"—along with the prophets of Baal and Asherah.

The populace gathered in silence. "I am the only one of the Lord's prophets left," Elijah informed them, "but Baal has four hundred and fifty prophets. Get two bulls for us. Let them choose one for themselves, and then cut it into pieces and put it on the wood but not set fire to it."

"I will prepare the other bull and put it on the wood but not set fire to it," he added. "Then you call on the name of your god, and I will call on the name of the Lord. The god who answers by fire—he is God." The populace was agreeable.

So it was that the prophets of Baal called on their deity from morning till noon. "O Baal, answer us!" they shouted. But there was no response, even though they worked themselves into a frenzy.

At noon the prophet of the Lord began to taunt them. "Shout louder!" he admonished them. "Surely he is god! Perhaps he is deep in thought, or busy, or traveling. Maybe he is sleeping and must be awakened." So they shouted louder, and slashed themselves with swords and spears—as was their custom, until their blood flowed.

Midday passed, and they continued their frantic attempts to incite Baal to action—until the time of the evening sacrifice. Whereupon, Elijah enjoined the people: "Come here to me." He repaired the altar of the Lord, arranged wood on it, and laid the sacrifice on top of the wood. "Fill four large jars with water and pour it on the offering and on the wood," he instructed those present. "Do it again," he directed them. "Do it a third time," he added. "Answer me, O Lord, answer me," he petitioned, "so these people will know that you, O Lord, are God, and that you are turning their hearts back again."

"Then the fire of the Lord fell and burned up the sacrifice, the wood, the stones and the soil, and also licked up the water in the trench." When the people saw this, they prostrated themselves, and confirmed: "The Lord—he is God! The Lord—he is God!"

In retrospect, "How composed and self-assured he is in contrast to the wild acrobatics of the Baal worshipers. . . . Among many lessons in the passage, one is primary: the impossibility of neutrality in relationship to God."[3]

A third ganglion embraces the life and ministry of Jesus, coupled with the acts of the apostles. Now there was a man named *Lazarus*, who was critically ill. Once Jesus and his disciples arrived at his home in Bethany, he was already in the tomb four days. "Lord," Martha addressed Jesus, "if you had been here, my brother would not have died. But I know that even now God will give you whatever you ask" (John 11:21-22).

Jesus replied, "Your brother will rise again."

Martha answered, "I know he will rise again in the resurrection at the last day."

"I am the resurrection and the life," Jesus informed her. "He who believes in me will live, even though he dies; and whoever lives and believes in me will never die."

When they had reached the tomb, Jesus instructed them to roll the stone away. "Father," he acknowledged, "I thank you that you have heard me. I knew that you always hear me, but I said this for the benefit of the people standing here, that they may believe that you sent me." When he had thus spoken, he called out in a loud voice: "Lazarus, come out!" The dead man came forth, his hands and feet still wrapped with strips of linen, and a cloth around his face. "Take off his grave clothes and let him go," Jesus instructed them.

On another occasion, I noted the implications of this miracle for Jesus' messianic claim. Initially, "It was known to Lazarus' associates. The report was not a matter of hearsay or some garbled tradition. Those best acquainted with the facts attested to the sign and its significance."[4]

Secondly, "It triggered the populace's support of Jesus." John presses the issue deftly: "So the multitude who were with him when he called Lazarus out of the tomb and raised him from the dead, were bearing him witness," and adds, "for this cause also the multitude went and met him, because they heard that he had performed this sign" (John 12:17-18).

Finally, "It initiated Gentile interest. John was not unmindful of the differences in religious background between Jews and their pagan neighbors. Time had already illustrated Jesus' appeal across religious/cultural boundaries, and John affirms that it was so from the beginning."

Is this rationale still plausible? Qualifications aside, it would seem so. In particular, John notes the blindness that plagues our human condition (12:4), and the pressure of society (12:42-43). As for the former, men love darkness rather than light—because of their evil disposition. As for the latter, one must tenaciously resist conformity to the world and what passes for social correctness.

Miracles continued to proliferate with the apostles. As noted earlier, a previous study concerned the activity of the Holy Spirit in Acts. "Was the miraculous constantly evident?" I rhetorically inquired. "No. In less than twenty instances, assuming a more generous interpretation of what qualifies, were extraordinary events reported. Likewise of interest, all but four of these instances were related to the apostles and might best be understood as attesting to their particular office."[5]

Conversely, forty of the forty-eight instances made reference to the faith community. This, in turn, recalls an incident I have appreciatively noted on other occasions. Helmut Thielicke tells of a time he shared communion with some Herero tribesmen. "They had never heard of our city, and I had known nothing of that remote bush country. Neither of us understand a single word of the others's language. But when I made the sign of the cross with my hand and pronounced the name 'Jesus' their dark faces lit up."[6] Whereupon, they could not do enough to show their love and devotion.

Now there was in Lystra a man crippled from birth. Fixing his eyes on him, Paul admonished: "Stand up on your feet!" (Acts 14:10). At that, the man jumped up and began to walk. When the populace saw this, they supposed that Paul and Barnabas were gods, and meant to sacrifice to them. "Men, why are you doing this?" they protested. "We too are only men, human like you." Even so, they had difficulty dissuading them from their idolatrous intent.

Then, when opposition arrived, the populace dragged the apostle outside the city, and stoned him—leaving him for dead. When he survived, he followed them back into the city. One can only speculate on the populace's response to seeing one thought to be dead walking in their midst. In any case, the apostle shortly took his leave.

Later on, Paul and Silas found themselves in Philippi. They went outside the city gate to the river, supposing that it might be a location for prayer—since there was no synagogue available. There they met Lydia, a merchant and God-fearing Gentile. "The Lord opened her heart to respond to Paul's message" (Acts 15:14). When she and her household were baptized, she invited the visitors to accept her hospitality.

Once when they were going to the place of prayer, they were met by a slave girl who earned a great deal of money for her owners by fortune-telling. The girl kept following them, shouting: "These men are servants of the Most High God, who are telling you the way to be saved." She continued to do so on subsequent occasions.

Finally, Paul became disturbed by this and rebuked the spirit: "In the name of Jesus Christ I command you to come out of her!" At which, the spirit complied. "The superior authority which such spirits had recognized when Jesus himself commanded them to leave their victims was equally recognized when his name was invoked by one of his disciples, and proved as potent in exorcism as in other forms of healing."[7]

When the owners realized that they had lost their means for making money, they were incensed and dragged Paul and Silas before the authorities. The populace joined in the incrimination, and they were flogged and cast into prison.

About midnight, they were praying and singing hymns, when suddenly there was a violent earthquake that shook the foundations of the prison. The jailor was understandably terrified, and asked what he must do to be saved. Paul seized on the opportunity to lead him to Christ. The prisoners were released the next day, and continued on their way—leaving a trail of miracles to bear witness to their ministry.

11

MORAL MYSTERY

One of the curious things about humans is that they have a sense of right and wrong, even though this differs from culture to culture, and person to person. For instance, a traditional village person may see nothing immodest about a woman with bare breasts. However, he or she does evidence a concern for modesty.

Morality has religious, social, and personal implications. "Do two walk together unless they have agreed to do so?" the Lord rhetorically inquires (Amos 3:3). Obviously not! Consequently, man is obligated to alter his ways to conform to that of the Almighty.

It is well to bear in mind Paul Tillich's observation that when human ideals supplant religious convictions, they serve as an alternative religion. He defines religion in terms of *ultimate concern*. In this regard, Jesus observed: "No one can serve two masters. Either he will hate the one and love the other, or he will be devoted to the one and despise the other. You cannot serve both God and Money" (Matt. 6:24). Here material acquisition is personified, as if an idol.

Morality is no less social in character. "Religion that God our Father accepts as pure and faultless is this: to look after orphans and widows in their distress and to keep oneself from being polluted by the world" (James 1:27). Ritual observances do not substitute for practical application.

By way of example, "was not Rahab the prostitute considered righteous for what she did when she gave lodging to the spies and sent them off in a different direction? As the body without the spirit is dead, so faith without deeds is dead" (2:25-26).

Then, too, morality is decidedly personal. "Love one another as I have loved you," Jesus enjoined his disciples. "Greater love has no one than this, that he lay down his life for his friends. " (John 15:12-13). As intimated earlier, Augustine admonished: "Love, and do what you will."[1]

Note also that *love* requires innovation, and not simply a slavish observance of some external code. Conversely, this is not meant to supplant sound instruction. I was reminded of this some years ago, when I inquired of a Jesuit priest his appraisal of situation ethics. He pointedly replied, "One needs guidelines to properly evaluate any given situation."

It remains to illustrate the moral mystery in select instances. With this in mind, we turn to the turbulent time of the Judges. "The Hebrew word *spt* has a broader semantic range than does the English term 'judge.' The Hebrew can also mean 'leader' or 'deliverer.' They were charismatic figures, divinely raised up in times of crisis."[2]

The text looks backward as well as forward, as evident from its introductory allusion, "After the death of Joshua." He "had fulfilled his mission on earth: Israel was one united people , completely settled in the promised land with 'rest' from enemies 'on every side,' in short, having realized 'all of the Lord's good promises to the house of Israel' (Joshua 21:44-45)."[3]

The future remained less certain, although a predictable cycle soon emerged. Initially, the people fall away from their covenant obligations. Unable to control the evil within, they could not contend with oppression from without. Whereupon, they cry out to the Lord in their desperation. In response, he sends them a deliverer. A time of peace ensues, during which the people become callous. The cycle then repeats itself.

Now Micah built a shrine, erected idols, and installed one of his sons as the family priest. "In those days Israel had no king; everyone did as he saw fit" (17:6). Previous to the separation of the tribe of Levi for priestly duties, "it is likely that (they) were fulfilled by the first-born. The by-passing of the Levitical priesthood by Micah may be due either to a break-down in the distribution of the Levites among the community or an overlooking, wilful or ignorant, of the provisions of the Law."[4]

Everyone did as he saw fit is tantamount to saying that a state of anarchy existed. The sense of morality had thus lost any semblance of social consensus. This allowed for a wide range of expedient behavior. It also brings to mind the adage, "Some order is better than none."

This thesis is borne out in a subsequent episode. By way of repetition, "In those days Israel had no king" (19:1). Implicit in this regard is that "everyone did as he saw fit." Now a Levite (notably absent in the above instance), who lived in a remote area in the hill country of Ephraim, took a concubine from Bethlehem of Judah. The practice of embracing a concubine was common in antiquity. The circumstances varied, so that it might simply be an economical means for gaining a wife—since no dowry would be required in the transaction.

However, she was unfaithful to him; a textual variant suggesting instead that she was angry with him. Assuming the former, there is no reason to suppose that her unfaithfulness took the form of adultery. It may simply imply that she decided to terminate their relationship. In any case, she remained with her father for four months, before her *husband* came in an attempt to persuade her return. It may have been that he was in hopes she would reconsider on her own, or be pressured to do so by her father.

His father-in-law welcomed the initiative, and prevailed upon him to remain for three days. After that, to extend his stay for another day. "The leisureliness of the East, particularly in connection with festive occasions showed itself in the hospitality pressed upon the Levite, whose attempt to return on the fourth day was completely thwarted."[5]

The morning of the fifth day, the girl's father urged him: "Refresh yourself. Wait till afternoon!" Once again he postponed his departure. Then, when he rose to leave, his father-in-law implored him to wait over to the next morning. But unwilling to stay another night, the man took his leave—along with his concubine, servant, and donkeys.

The day was far spent when they arrived in the vicinity of Jebus (Jerusalem). "Come," his servant urged him, "let's stop at this city of the Jebusites and spend the night."

"No," the Levite insisted. "We won't go into an alien city, whose people are not Israelites. We will go on to Gibeah." This was in anticipation of receiving preferable treatment.

Upon arriving at their destination, "They went and sat in the city square, but no one took them into his home for the night." This failure to offer hospitality, which was considered a sacred duty, served as an ominous warning of things yet to come.

That evening an elderly man from the country of Ephraim, who was living in Gibeah, came in from the fields where he was working. "Let me supply whatever you need," he enjoined them. "Only don't spend the night in the square." So he took them into his home.

While they were refreshing themselves, some of *the wicked men* of the city surrounded the house. "Bring out the man who came to your house so we can have sex with him," they demanded.

The elderly man went outside to reason with them. "No, my friends," he admonished them, "don't be so vile." Instead, he offered his virgin daughter and the Levite's concubine to satisfy their sexual lusts. While commentators are quick to point out that this reveals a relative disregard for women, the counter-proposal also suggests an abhorrence of homosexual behavior.

In any case, the wicked men settled for gang raping and abusing the concubine throughout the night, and at dawn let her go. She dragged herself back to the house of their host, and fell down at the door—where she lay until daylight. When the Levite opened the door, he found her lifeless body.

Upon reaching home, he took a knife and cut up his concubine into twelve parts and sent them as a gruesome reminder throughout the land of what had transpired. Then the Israelites came out *as one man* against the Benjamanites, since they refused to surrender those guilty of the infraction. The slaughter was so great that the tribe was threatened with extinction. All things considered, "In those days Israel had no king; everyone did as he saw fit" (21:25).

There follows the rise and fall of the monarchy, exile, the return of a remnant, and birth pains of the messianic era. A remarkable personage from Galilee makes his appearance. Persons are first impressed by the authoritative character of his message, quite unlike the practice of relying on religious precedent. Then, too, he performs in astonishing ways, such as healing the infirm and exorcism.

The moral implication of his message was summed up in the succinct summons: "Come, follow me." "Only three words, they speak a volume. . . . The implications were staggering. In military terms, He offered high ground not previously available."[6]

By way of example, Jesus was passing through Jericho when he saw a man named *Zacchaeus*, curiously looking down on him from the limb of a sycamore-fig tree. "Zacchaeus, come down immediately," Jesus called out to him. "I must stay at your house today" (Luke 19:5). So he gladly welcomed Jesus.

When the populace observed this, they complained: "He has gone to be the guest of a 'sinner' (non-observant Jew)."

"Look, Lord!" Zacchaeus protested. "Here and now I give half of my possessions to the poor, and if I have cheated anybody out of anything, I will pay back four times the amount." Such as would require a serious moral commitment.

All else might be construed as commentary. Initially, it should be pointed out that "the direct and immediate source of moral responsibility is the free will of man which can be considered . . . only in the light of (his) knowledge of values, his own inner disposition and spirit, his own conscience."[7] Genuine freedom consists of being able to make decisions in the light of relevant information, and inner rectitude.

The stakes are high when it comes to exercising freedom. As with the original couple, but also with their posterity. Our choices have lingering effects, although God minimizes the influence of sin, while maximizing the consequence of good. By way of confirmation, the Lord punishes "the sin of the fathers to the third and fourth generation of those who hate (him), but shows love to a thousand generations of those who love (him) and keep (his) commandments" (Exodus 5-6).

"The will of God is not left in general terms; the particular aspect of his will that Jesus came to perform has to do with what the Father gives him."[8] So also with others, each according to his or her calling, at an appropriate time, in concert with others—to the glory of the Almighty.

Accordingly, Jesus taught his disciples to pray: "your will be done on earth as it is in heaven" (Matt. 6:10). This was in keeping with his own example, as echoed by the petition: "My Father, if it is not possible for this cup to be taken away unless I drink it, may your will be done" (Matt. 26:42). *God's will* must be realized in varied situations. For Jesus, it involved crucifixion. For some, it has meant leaving their familiar surroundings, to serve in the mission field. For still others, it requires taking seriously the obligation to raise their children in the ways of the Lord.

Whatever the particular circumstances, it embodies death to oneself and life in Christ. Death to all that we might have desired, whether good or bad. Life to all that following Jesus may entail, both adversity and blessing.

How is one to know the will of God? Essentially through a transformation of one's way of thinking, as nurtured by a ready acceptance of biblical teaching—coupled with earnest prayer. So also through the counsel of others, and the experiences of life.

As often said, the would-be follower of Jesus must be *in* the world, but not *of* the world. Jesus was no recluse. Nor did he seek sanctuary among the religious elite. Conversely, he did not succumb to the depravity that surrounded him. In doing so, he provided a divine leverage to extricate others from their futility.

William Wilberforce comes to mind in this connection. "No proponent for the abolition of slavery ever accomplished more. Largely as a result of his indefatigable efforts, slavery came to a complete end in all of the British Empire's possessions by 1840, making it the first modern country to outlaw slavery."[9]

The call to follow Jesus was no less a call to community. As graphically expressed, when one finds his or her way to the cross, there are others knelt around him or her. From this time on, the convert is meant to live in reciprocal relationships with others of like precious faith. So also by being open individually and corporately to God's leading.

I recall in this connection the practice of Elm-Lasalle Street Church in Chicago. Participants were encouraged to submit likely service projects, requiring community support. For instance, one concerned providing a legal service for youths who were encountering difficulty with the law. These projects were carefully prioritized, and general funds provided for those thought most urgent. Once the project was able to manage on its own, the support was shifted to another.

As the early Christian community expanded, it did so along the Roman network of connecting roadways. Consequently, it was primarily associated with urban centers. These accommodated a variety of ethnic people, and differing customs. They were also more open to change.

This was in some measure a passing phenomenon, since the faith having taken root in an urban environ, soon expanded into the surrounding region. This served to substantiate the cosmopolitan character of the faith, and give credence to its claim for universal acceptance. It also accented the importance of identification with the larger community. Accordingly, Paul admonishes: "Give everyone what you owe him. If you owe taxes, pay taxes; if revenue, then revenue; if respect; then respect; if honor, then honor" (Rom. 13:7). Since it is deemed the right thing to do, in keeping with a Christian perception of accountability. Sufficient to say, "God wills it!"

12

ENIGMAS: PART ONE

The biblical text itself is beset with enigma. As a consequence, we are often hard put to explain one passage or another. It is not simply that we have difficulty coming up with a plausible answer, but may not even know what question to ask. The following discussion will illustrate this thesis. (The symbol "~"will signify a new topic.)

~ The instance that initially comes to mind concerns attributing the Pentateuch to Moses, rather than a complex theory of reconstruction dating essentially to a later period. The internal evidence would appear to support the former. For instance, then the Lord enjoined Moses, "Write this on a scroll as something to be remembered and make sure that Joshua hears it, because I will completely blot out the memory of Malek from under heaven" (Exodus 14). So also Jesus observed, "If you believed Moses, you would believe me, for he wrote about me" (John 5:46).

There is considerable corroborating evidence as well. As an example, "The trees and animals referred to in Exodus through Deuteronomy are all indigenous to Egypt or the Sinai Peninsula, but none of them are peculiar to Palestine. The shittim or acacia tree is native to Egypt and the Sinai, but it is hardly found in Canaan except around the Dead Sea."[1]

In conclusion, although much new information has been gathered, "the discoveries have not ended the debate about the authorship of the Pentateuch. Yet at the same time the case for the Mosaic authorship has been strengthened by our increasing knowledge about the history, culture, and religion of the ancient Near East."[2] Then, too, this does not preclude the possibility that the text draws on other sources, by way of formulating its account of human beginnings and the patriarchal period.

~ A related question concerns how the Genesis account can be reconciled with evidence from fossils and fissionable minerals in the geological strata that point to an exceedingly early origin for the earth. While the term *yom* can be employed for an indefinite period of time, the addition of the expression *there was evening and there was morning*—while not conclusive—gives the impression of a twenty-four hour time span. Even so, one need not conclude that these days were consecutive.

The evolution controversy often generates more heat than light when it comes to this and similar issues. It would be helpful to distinguish between limited evolution— such as can be documented, and comprehensive evolution—which is better relegated to the realm of philosophy. Some years ago the distinguished biologist Russell Mixter graphically illustrated how the record of evolution had run its course before considering how the various prototype species were initiated. At that point, he suggested one may opt for natural or supernatural means. He thought that the latter was more likely.

~ Now Abel kept flocks, while Cain worked the soil. In the course of time, the former brought fat portions from the firstborn of his flock for an offering, whereas the latter provided indiscriminate fruits of the soil. "The Lord looked with favor on Abel and his offering, but on Cain and his offering he did not look with favor" (Gen. 4:4-5). The reason for this is not explicitly mentioned.

Not surprising, some pick up on the fact that Abel offered a blood sacrifice. In this regard, "without the shedding of blood there is no forgiveness" (Heb. 9:22). It, however, seems more likely that Abel's sacrifice was more along the line of that offered to an honored guest, while Cain's was an ordinary sort—showing a lack of deference.

~ "Altogether," we are told, "Adam lived 930 years, and then he died" (Gen. 5:5). This, in turn, recalls the comment of my maternal grandmother. When observed that she could live to be a hundred, she replied: "Yes, but would it be worth it?" She was well along in life at the time.

The simplest answer to the question why in antiquity persons lived longer is that there was some residual effects from man's original state—so that their health and vigor were relatively unimpaired. Worthy of note, life expectancy seems to have significantly depreciated after the flood. "The length of our days is seventy years," as previously observed, "or eighty, if we have the strength; yet their span is but trouble and sorrow, for they quickly pass, and we fly away" (90:10).

~ As concerns the flood, the waters "rose greatly on the earth, and all the high mountains under the entire heavens were covered" (Gen. 7:19). Some argue for an universal flood while others for a local alternative. While the former may be preferred, this could be a reference to the observable world. In any case, we should not interpret the term *all* as universal if it appears that restrictions are intended.

"If the Flood was global, the number of miracles involved were greater than if it was local, but either way the miraculous is clearly evident throughout the account. The issue is not what *could* God have done, but what *did* he do in the great catastrophe."[3] It is quite possible that if we were to know the actual conditions, they would appear stranger still.

~ "Now the whole world had one language and a common speech. . . . Come (they said to one another), let us build ourselves a city, with a tower that reaches to the heavens, so that we may make a name for ourselves and not be scattered over the face of the whole earth" (Gen. 11:1, 4). Seeing their presumption and recognizing its danger, God confused their language—so that as a consequence, they were scattered over all the earth.

Some have proposed that this corresponds to a documented time when the common language was disrupted by an incursion of alien people, which would obviously argue for a more local phenomena. In any case, "The fact that they continued to maintain their integrity according to their lineage strongly suggests that each of these smaller subdivisions was allowed a language mutually comprehensible to those within the clan, even after the confusion of tongues at Babel."[4] So the situation has continued.

~ Persons may be unduly concerned over such conventional expressions as "when the sun went down" (Gen. 15:17), supposing they are in conflict with scientific data. This brings to mind C. S. Lewis' caution, "Likely an immature person should not read a book meant for mature individuals." Accordingly, he meant that we understand the text on its own terms rather than imposing something extraneous.

To state what should be obvious, this is simply a common manner of speaking. As such, the sun appears to have sunk below the horizon—albeit this is not meant as a cosmic explanation. Furthermore, we continue to speak along these lines—with the rising and setting of the sun.

~ "You are to undergo circumcision," God informed Abram (Abraham), "and it will be the sign of the covenant between me and you" (Gen. 17:11). The text does not furnish any clear rationale for this ritual, other than it was prescribed by the Almighty. Consequently, it would be a distinguishing mark for the covenant people.

It is also alleged that circumcision serves to reduce health risks. While disputed by a recent study, it is solely for this reason that some persons opt for the practice.

~ Genesis concludes with the Israelites having found sanctuary in Egypt, and Exodus opens with their numbers greatly increased—thus posing a threat to the Egyptian dynasty. Moses takes center stage, as God's means for delivering his chosen people. Having fled from the country under duress, he perhaps seems an unlikely choice. However, God knows the end from the beginning.

We do well to bear this in mind when reading the text. What comes as something of a surprise at the moment, falls into place in retrospect. Accordingly, there is a pattern to God's working, as obscure as it may appear at the time.

~ Now "Aaron threw his staff down in front of Pharaoh and his officials, and it became a snake. Pharaoh then summoned wise men and sorcerers, and the Egyptian magicians also did the same things by their secret arts" (Exodus 7:10-11). Some reason that the magicians accomplished their feat by way of evil powers, citing as confirmation: "The coming of the lawless one will be in accordance with the work of Satan displayed in all kinds of counterfeit miracles, signs and wonder" (2 Thess. 2:9).

Conversely, they may have shown "a skill not much different from that of professional magicians today, who know how to produce rabbits or doves out of their hats. Their staffs that turned into serpents when cast on the ground may have been snakes that they had charmed into rigidity."[5]

~ As mentioned in an earlier context, the plagues are variously accounted for. As an example, "The blood-red coloring has been attributed to an excess of both red earth and the bright red algae with its bacteria (both which accompany flooding). Rather than the abundant life usually brought by the river, this brought death to the fish and detriment to the soil."[6]

However one might seek to explain such phenomena, their timing and immensity seem out of proportion to all known criteria. Accordingly, there has been an attempt to tie them to a volcanic eruption in the Aegean Sea. In any case, the writer wants us to know that God was at work in what transpired. This leaves the impression that what is impossible with man can be implemented by the Almighty.

~ Another thorny problem confronting the reader is the staggering size of the Israelite nation as they made their way out of Egypt. "There were about six hundred thousand men on foot, besides women and children" (Exodus 12:37). "Many other people also went along with them," constituting a sizable assembly. Providing, that is, that the numbers be taken literally, since some speculate that the term *thousand* should be understood as idiomatic for a large number. In some instances, this appears to be the case, although it is not certain that this is one of them.

A literal interpretation would represent a dramatic increase in the size of the populace over a relatively short span of time. This would certainly be in keeping with the concern expressed by Pharaoh regarding the phenomenal Israelite growth, and likely threat this constituted for a dynasty vulnerable to incursion from outside.

As a related matter, it would be virtually inconceivable that one could sustain such a multitude over an extended time in the wilderness. Conversely, the provision of manna would speak to this need. Further speculation would in any case seem pointless.

~ Several compatible rationales have been set forth by way of explaining the distinction between clean and unclean in the Levitical Code. In some instances, it appears intended to set the chosen people apart from pagan religious practices. As an example, the pig was employed in Canaanite worship. Moreover, it carried parasitic organisms injurious to health, especially trichinosis. As for the prohibition against eating shellfish, it is thought that this might be in lieu of the Israelites sojourn in the Delta region of Egypt, where this was said to be a problem.

Clean animals were also meant to conform to what was thought normal for their species. Accordingly, "Holiness requires that individuals shall conform to the class to which they belong. And holiness requires that different classes of things shall not be confused."[7]

Finally, the rabbis concluded that certain instances were intended merely to accent the distinctive character of the chosen people. These were not arbitrary in the strict sense of the word, since they were deliberately chosen to accentuate the peculiar identity of the people. As such, it was not only an evidence to others, but a reminder to themselves.

~ While the Mosaic Covenant was once thought to have no precedent, it now appears to follow the pattern of a vassal treaty. In particular, it consists of an introduction, historical prologue, stipulations, sanctions, and provision for covenant renewal. The *introduction* focuses on the sovereign majesty of the Almighty, and the historical *prologue* recounts some of his faithful exploits.

The *stipulations* constitute the bulk of the text. These contain both *apodictic* and *casuistic law*. The former consists of broad general principles, while the latter amounts to case applications.

The *sanctions* are set forth in terms of blessing and cursing, depending on whether persons abide by their covenant obligation. After which, the *covenant renewal* regulates the manner in which the covenant may be confirmed. This implies a sustained commitment to the covenant, while deftly adapting to changing circumstances. In this regard, we are again reminded that *mystery* consists not in something altogether unfathomable, but that which becomes more clear with the passing of time.

~ While there was no general prohibition against the use of wine, Scripture abounds with warnings concerning its consumption. As an especially interesting instance, the Lord instructed Aaron: "You and your sons are not to drink wine or other fermented drink whenever you go into the Tent of Meeting, or you will die" (Lev. 10:9). Then, by way of explanation: "You must distinguish between the holy and common, between the unclean and clean, and you must teach the Israelites all the decrees the Lord has given them through Moses."

"This prohibition obviously stresses the need for the priests to be clearheaded when leading in Worship. Some suggest that it was a reminder not to indulge in the worship of the religions around them, in which alcohol was often used as a stimulus to false worship."[8] A similar line of reasoning could readily apply to enjoining people not to drink before driving an automobile.

While we have barely scratched the surface of textual enigmas, we will conclude this initial discussion at this juncture. Subsequently, we will pick up with the New Testament by way of exploring the topic still further. It would seem evident even from this brief incursion that there is merit in the adage, "The more we know, the more we realize we do not know." Accordingly, ambiguity is alive and well in the biblical text.

13

ENIGMAS: PART II

The trail of textual enigmas manifestly extends into the New Testament. It thus revolves around the life and ministry of Jesus, and the extended activity of the apostolic circle. A few representative examples will suffice to serve our current purposes.

~ It is commonly thought the Old and New Testaments portray a very different deity. As for the former, he is said to be jealous, wrathful, and vindictive. The latter is cast in a much more favorable light: as compassionate, forgiving, and merciful.

Of course, this is to overstate the alleged contrast. For instance, "As the father has compassion on his children, so the Lord has compassion on those who fear him" (Psa. 103:13). Moreover, the covenant should be understood as an expression of God's lavish grace, rather than something merited.

Conversely, "The wrath of God is being revealed from heaven against all the godlessness and wickedness of men who suppress the truth by their wickedness, since what is known about God is plain to them, because God has made it plain to them" (Rom. 1:8). Then, too, Jesus experienced God's wrath in vicarious manner—so as to redeem man from his sin. Accordingly, it would appear that the portrait of God is consistent through the biblical text, given the progress in salvation history.

~ What is one to make of the similarities and differences among the Synoptic Gospels: Matthew, Mark, and Luke? This usually invokes some sort of documentary hypothesis. Its most common option consists of identifying Mark and Q (standing for a no longer existent manuscript) as the original sources. However, others insist that Luke was the original—on the basis of linguistic analysis.

In any case, one ought not to overlook the importance of oral transmission. The word was passed on from one person to the next, until compiled in an acceptable manner. Even if this factor does not serve as a likely substitute for the documentary hypothesis, it should be coupled together with it—to provide a more comprehensive explanation.

Of course, each of the individual gospels reflects a somewhat distinctive agenda. As an example, "Luke came to his task from the perspective of an educated Greek, a physician who took a special interest in the details of Christ's miracles of healing."[1] He also attempted to set forth *an orderly account* of Jesus' life and ministry. As a result, the events with one or two exceptions might be chronological. Much interest is likewise devoted to Jesus' interaction with women and children, and his recourse to prayer at critical moments. This constitutes only a short list.

~ How is one to explain the pronounced differences between Jesus' genealogy in Matthew and Luke? Likely the most prominent options, "(1) one (probably Matthew) records the genealogy of Joseph; (2) one (probably Matthew) spiritualizes the genealogy; (3) the lines of descent cross but are different because one list includes several lines through levirate marriages (Deut. 25:5-10)."[2] Then, too, a literary accommodation might better serve instead of the an obscure reference to spiritualizing the passage.

In any case, it was important to establish Jesus' Davidic lineage. In this regard, two blind men followed Jesus, calling out to him: "Have mercy on us, Son of David!" (Matt. 9:27).

"Do you believe that I am able to do this?" he inquired.

"Yes, Lord," they replied.

"According to your faith will it be done to you," he answered, and they were able to see. All of this was in keeping with Jesus' role as the Messiah.

~ Some ambiguity surrounds the pilgrimage of the Magi to welcome the birth of Jesus. The prophets discouraged astrology, especially in the context of its idolatrous practice. As such, it was thought to circumvent God's guidance.

Conversely, there was no idolatrous intent expressed in their visit. By way of explanation, "Jupiter was regarded as the star of the ruler of the universe, and the constellation of the Fishes as the sign for the last days. In the East, Saturn was considered to be the planet of Palestine."[3] If Jupiter were to encounter Saturn in the sign of the Fishes, it would signify that the latter day ruler was about to appear in Palestine. Meanwhile, the Magi wasted no time in trying to locate him.

They joined other unlikely recipients of the good news, such as a girl from Nazareth—thought not important enough to be previously mentioned in Holy Writ, religiously non-observant shepherds, and subsequently to a host of unlikely individuals. Notably absent were the religious elite, who prided themselves on their privileged access to the Almighty.

~ How are we to understand Jesus' temptations in light of James' assertion that "each one is tempted when, by his own evil desire, he is dragged away and enticed" (1:14)? The point that James is making is that persons are responsible for their own inclination and behavior. Accordingly, they should not lay the blame on the Almighty

As for Jesus, he was "tempted in every way, just as we are—yet was without sin" (Heb. 4:15). Qualifications aside, it would appear that a righteous resolve would intensify temptation—in that the conflict would be exaggerated. If this is an accurate assessment, then Jesus found the experience eminently more difficult than others.

~ Why was Jesus inclined to refer to himself by the relatively obscure designation *the Son of Man*? As noted previously, the messianic tradition sometimes depicted God intervening personally and on other occasions in terms of an emissary. These strands coalesce in Jesus. In particular, it accented his common lot with humanity.

"In my vision at night I looked," Daniel recounts, "and there before me was one like a son of man, coming with the clouds of heaven" (7:13). When the expression is used in its ordinary sense, there is a dignity implied—in keeping with man being created in God's image. However, "the visionary setting introduces new elements. The seer has been lifted above the earth and is able to discern amid the clouds of heaven the judgement-throne of God. In these unfamiliar surroundings he (meant to say that) the one he saw was *like* a son of man."[4] As with regard to the three animals, he was likened to his earthly counterparts.

~ "I tell you the truth," Jesus solemnly declared, "some who are standing here will not taste death before they see the Son of Man coming in his kingdom" (Matt. 16:28). Since Jesus explicitly indicates that no one knows the precise time of the consummation, it is likely that he meant to refer to some interim event. "Of the various suggestions offered, the two that seem most possible are that Jesus will shortly be transfigured and that (he) speaks of the intermediate kingdom of Christ in and through his church."[5]

In support of the latter alternative, Jesus assured his disciples: "I will not leave you as orphans, I will come to you" (John 14:16). In context, it would appear that he spoke concerning the outpouring of the Spirit.

~ The manner in which the Old Testament is quoted has long been a topic of discussion. As an example, Jeremiah is credited with saying: "They took the thirty silver coins, the price set on him by the people of Israel, and they used them to buy the potter's field, as the Lord commanded" (Matt. 27:9-10). In brief, assigning a composite quotation to the more prominent individual seems to have been a common practice.

In greater detail, Jeremiah is told to go down to the potter's house, and buy a field in Anathoth; whereas Zechariah is paid thirty pieces of silver, which he cast into the house of the potter. "Following a method of exegesis that falls strangely on the ears of a modern interpreter, this collection of ideas is understood to have been fulfilled by events leading up to the purchase of a burial place for foreigners with blood money supplied by Judas' suicide."[6]

~ Now there appears to be a discrepancy between the Synoptic report that Jesus was crucified at the *third* hour (cf. Mark 15:25), and John's observation that his trial was still in process at the *sixth* hour (cf. John 19:14). Nevertheless, the problem disappears if we assume that John was employing the official Roman system of numbering—rather than the cultural manner assumed by the other writers.

This, understandably, raises the question why John would be inclined to deviate. The answer likely comes from the time and location in which the fourth gospel was recorded. If, as some suppose, it originated in Ephesus—this served as the capital of the Roman province of Asia. It would therefore seem natural to employ the Roman means of recording, if for no other reason than to facilitate communication.

~ One would gather that Jesus was crucified on Friday except for the before-mentioned text in John that identifies it as *the day of Preparation of Passover Week.* In this connection, it should be observed that the notion of *preparation* had come to serve in a technical sense for Friday—as preparatory for the Sabbath observance. Then, too, the *Passover* is construed as extending to the seven-day Feast of Unleavened Bread.

It would thus appear that John affirms just as clearly as the Synoptic Gospels that Christ was crucified on Friday, and then to be raised on the first day of the week. This, of course, assumes an idiomatic usage— in which any portion qualifies as a day. This means of expression is borne out in the three day interval before which Esther approached the king on the third day (cf. Esther 4:16-5:1).

~ Early on in my seminary training I came across the conclusion that there was no way to reconcile the various accounts of the resurrection appearances. At this, I sat down at my desk to construct a plausible harmony. It proved not to be all that difficult an exercise.

Meanwhile, it became evident that there was a common point of reference throughout. This was all the more impressive given the various perspectives that were brought to bear. Needless to say, the resurrection narratives were indelibly written on the collective memory of the early fellowship.

~ The disciples were subsequently enjoined to tarry until they were endued with "power when the Holy Spirit comes to you, and you will be my witnesses to Jerusalem, and in all Judea and Samaria, and to the ends of the earth" (Acts 1:8). This *power* might pertain to a personal boldness, effective ministry, or some combination of the two.

When the day of Pentecost had arrived, they were all together in one place—suggesting a common purpose. Suddenly there was a sound like the blowing of a violent wind that filled the house where they were sitting. Then they saw what seemed to be tongues of fire that separated and came to rest on each of them. All were filled with the Holy Spirit, and all or some of them began to speak in tongues other than their common dialect.

It bears repeating that this was reminiscent of God manifesting himself in former times. As on the occasion when the Lord appeared to Elijah upon his reaching Horeb, *the mountain of God* (cf. 1 Kings 19:9-18). "Go out and stand on the mountain in the presence of the Lord," God commanded him, "for the Lord is about to pass by."

"Then a great and powerful wind tore the mountains apart and showered the rocks before the Lord, but the Lord was not in the wind. After the wind there was an earthquake, but the Lord was not in the earthquake. After the earthquake came a fire, but the Lord was not in the fire." All of these were preparatory for the encounter with the Almighty, as if harbingers of that which was to come.

"And after the fire came a gentle whisper." When the prophet heard the whisper, he pulled his cloak over his face and went out and stood at the mouth of the cave. Then God instructed him what he was to do next.

The parallel between this and the pouring out of the Spirit appears striking. God announces his presence, after which he confirms it. It remains to carry out his mission; in proverbial terms, "Come hell or high water."

~ Are the heathen genuinely lost? Paul makes it eminently clear that there are no exceptions. Is there then any hope for those who have not heard the gospel during their life time? Here we may have to reserve judgment.

Take the case of a Nigerian friend, who was raised in the home of a traditional village priest. He would on occasion help his father prepare a sacrifice to be offered at the sacred tree. One day he became critically ill. His parents relied on village medicine and religious ritual to attempt a cure, all to no avail.

Accordingly, they heard that *a man of God* was traveling through the region. This designation was reserved for those who serve the High God, said to be sovereign over all else. He came in response to the parents' request, and interceded on behalf of the youngster—who quickly began to mend.

The lad reasoned that the High God had some special purpose for his life. However, by definition the High God is inscrutable and unpredictable. While quite willing to cooperate, he was unaware how to do so.

He then encountered *an orange skin*, since his skin resembled that of the inside of an orange. The stranger informed him, "For God so loved the world that he gave his one and only Son, that whoever believes in him shall not perish but have eternal life" (John 3:16). Now whenever the term *God* was used in the singular, it was understood to be a reference to the High God.

Moreover, it was thought that one's son reveals his father's character. This being the case, he would learn what God desired of him. When I encountered this engaging person, he was teaching on a mission compound. What, however, if his life were terminated before hearing the assurance of salvation? Can we be certain, or is this also shrouded with mystery?

14

CREATIVE MYSTERY

Creativity has solicited extended study in a wide range of educational disciplines. Obviously, it does not entail creating something out of nothing. It has rather to do with fashioning something for functional and/or aesthetic reasons. As such, it is highly prized as a critical means of resolving persisting problems, and realizing new opportunities.

"The Lord God took the man and put him in the Garden of Eden to work it and take care of it" (Gen. 2:15). Man had only his God-given ingenuity to fashion tools, enabling him to fulfill his obligations. While there was a river watering the garden, some provision would have to be made for distribution. If one were unfamiliar with irrigation techniques, this would be a formidable challenge.

Conversely, the situation lent itself to creative endeavor. The inhibiting factors which we take for granted were largely absent. In popular idiom, man was conditioned to think *outside the box*—in an imaginative and productive manner.

Adam had no need for the complex farming equipment of today, since his was a modest enterprise. The situation would change, but with humans less alert as to how best to cope. In this regard, a world created by a benevolent deity, and containing creatures made in his image, "leads to the formation of people nurtured by God, capable of producing a few individuals of satisfactory spiritual nature, but in the main those who are obtuse, unfaithful, and frequently backsliding from the divinely given task."[1]

Language is a prime indication of man's creative potential. It allows him the opportunity to refer to things which occurred in the past, to anticipate future eventualities, and decide among available options. This occurs in a social context, where ideas can be readily shared.

All this differs from one culture to the next. As in the case of a traditional culture that was generally tolerant of deviant behavior, such as an agitated villager waving his spear in a threatening fashion. However, this tolerance did not extend to persons who were continually amicable, because it appeared contrived. Consequently, a missionary striving to maintain an even temperament would be viewed with suspicion.

Not all creative endeavors are praiseworthy. As humans moved eastward, they discovered an inviting plain and settled there. "Come," they encouraged one another, "let's make bricks and bake them thoroughly. Come, let us build ourselves a city, with a tower that reaches to the heavens, so that we may make a nation for ourselves and not be scattered over the face of the whole earth" (Gen. 11:3-4).

"They used brick instead of stone," the writer notes, "and tar for mortar." "The technology of baking brick was developed toward the end of the fourth millennium, and the resulting product, using bitumen as a mastic, proved waterproof and as sturdy as stone. Since it was an expensive process, it was used only for important public buildings."[2] This determination was no doubt reached after deliberate experimentation.

God frustrated this presumptive effort, lest something worse were to derive from it. He did so by confusing their language, so that they could not readily converse with one another. Whereupon, they were scattered abroad, and less tempted to assume divine prerogatives. Thus concludes a dismal chapter in human history.

Creativity is expressed in many ways. On one occasion, the Lord enjoined Abram (Abraham): "Leave your country, your people, and your father's household and go the land I will show you" (Gen. 12:1). This entailed leaving and fashioning a new life in unfamiliar surroundings.

The series of exhortations were increasingly threatening: from *your country*, *your people*, and *your father's household*. On the other hand, "I will make you into a great nation and I will bless you. I will make your name great, and you will be a blessing. I will bless those who bless you and whoever curses you I will curse, and all peoples on earth will be blessed through you." It would thus appear that when creativity is involved, the stakes can be high—not only for the individual but for others impacted.

The patriarch's experience also invites us to reflect on the creative process in greater detail. "It begins with the *amorphous stage*. (This corresponds to) the potter('s) lump of clay. For a writer, it consists of a blank monitor."[3]

Accordingly, "By faith Abraham, when called to go to a place he would later receive as his inheritance, obeyed and went, even though he did not know where he was going" (Heb. 11:8). "Now faith (by way of clarification) is being sure of what we hope for and certain of what we do not see" (v. 1).

Imagination is an indispensable component. It "opens doors that are normally closed. Through its power we sneak into forbidden situations, we explore terrifying territory, we try out new styles."[4] Imagination *opens doors*, thus allowing us to see beyond. This is sometimes by way of indirection. As an example, Albert Einstein initiated his study of relativity by imagining what things would look like if he traveled on a beam of light. After that, one thing led to another.

From a different perspective, it also allows us to *sneak into forbidden situations*. In other words, it incites us to defy convention. As sometimes expressed, to think the unthinkable, and do the undoable.

In a still different light, imagination encourages us to *explore terrifying territory*. As when a traditional person perceives a distant land as inhabited by strange people and fierce creatures. In this connection, they seemingly project their own insecurities.

Meanwhile, it entices us to *try new styles*. As an example, Paul aptly observes: "You were taught with regard to your former way of life, to put off your old self, which is being corrupted by its deceitful desires, to be made new in the attitude of your minds, and to put on the new self, created to be like God in true righteousness and holiness" (Eph. 4:22-24). This is represented as a single act, by which one turns from a reprehensible lifestyle to a constructive alternative.

"So Abram left," forebodings aside and in confidence that God would reward his efforts. The *initial step* in any creative enterprise is calculated to solicit grave misgivings. In particular, "We are reluctant to commit ourselves to an endeavor that may prove fruitless. Then, too, to invoke the criticism of others. If not, then an apathetic response."[5]

By way of illustration, the contingent sent out by Moses to reconnoiter the promised land reported back: "We went into the land to which you sent us, and it does flow with milk and honey! But the people who live there are powerful, and the cities are fortified and very large" (Num. 13:27-28). The people were intimidated by their appraisal, and thereby lost a golden opportunity. As a result, one generation perished before another would occupy the land.

Once a creative endeavor is initiated, it must be *verified*. "Now there was a famine in the land, and Abram went down to Egypt to live there for a while because the famine was severe" (Gen. 12:10). This was meant to be a temporary accommodation, until the situation were to take a turn for the better.

Meanwhile, he was concerned that the Egyptians would seize his attractive wife, and dispose of him. Accordingly, he prompted her to pose as his sister. When the desirable woman was brought to Pharaoh's attention, he had her brought to the palace. When the patriarch's deceit became known, the ruler sent them away. In terms of conventional wisdom, "All is well that ends well."

Taking leave of the patriarch, we pick up with the prophet Jeremiah. The word of the Lord came to him, saying: "Go down to the potter's house, and there I will give you my message" (Jer. 18:1). As noted earlier, the *potter* serves as a prime analogy for God's creative activity, so that the prophet may have anticipated that the Lord would speak to him along that line.

"So I went down to the potter's house, and I saw him working at the wheel. But the pot he was shaping from the clay was marred in his hands, so the potter formed it into another pot, shaping it as seemed best to him." Since the first creative endeavor was not satisfactory, he would attempt another.

"O house of Israel, can I not do with you as this potter does?" the Almighty inquires. "If at any time I announce that a nation or kingdom is to be uprooted, torn down and destroyed, and if that nation I warned repents of its evil, then I will relent and not inflict on it the disaster I had planned." Providing that it is pliable, as is the clay.

This, in turn, recalls a memorable instance when visiting a Hebron potter. He was appreciatively referred to as *the old man*, out of deference to the wisdom he had accumulated over the years. A number of persons stood about, waiting to observe his artistry. He paused momentarily, as if to visualize his project. Silence reigned.

The potter's wheel began to turn, and as if by magic a jug began to rise from a lump of clay. There was a murmur of appreciation from those assembled. They glanced knowingly at one another, with the trace of a smile gracing each face. In another setting, there might have been applause.

He soon set aside the finished product. This provided me with the opportunity to compare it with other samples of his creative artistry. No two were exactly the same, each being distinctive.

Creative inferences appear time and again in the biblical text. "The range of the apostolic message has been steadily broadened. Already it has begun to cross the barrier which separated Jews from Gentiles; now the time has come for that barrier to be crossed authoritatively by an apostle."[6] Peter was praying when he fell into a trance, and saw what resembled a sheet descending from heaven—with a variety of creatures therein. "Get up, Peter," he heard a voice saying. "Kill and eat" (Acts 10:13).

"Surely not Lord!" he protested. "I have never eaten anything impure or unclean."

"Do not call anything impure that God has made clean," the voice countered. This happened three times, before the sheet was taken back up into heaven. While the apostle was still reflecting on the significance of this vision, emissaries from the centurion Cornelius arrived. Now Cornelius revered the Almighty, and was prompted by an angel to solicit the apostle's services.

The next day Peter, along with the emissaries and some of the brothers from Joppa, set out for Caesarea. The apostle greeted Cornelius, and a large gathering of Gentiles intent on hearing what he would say. "You are well aware that it is against our law for a Jew to associate with a Gentile or visit him," the reluctant apostle allowed. "But God has shown me that I should not call any man impure or unclean." "I now realize how true it is that God does not show favoritism," he continued, "but accepts men from every nation who fear him and do what is right."

While Peter was still speaking, the Holy Spirit came on all who heard the message. The Jewish believers were astonished that Gentiles were implicated. "Can anyone keep these people from being baptized with water?" the apostle inquired. So they were baptized on profession of their faith.

When this became public knowledge, Peter was required to give an accounting of his deviant behavior. When those in Jerusalem heard what had transpired, "they had no further objections and praised God, saying: 'So then, God has granted even the Gentiles repentance unto life'" (Acts 11:18). This proved to be an important milestone in reaching out to all nations, in keeping with the great commission.

Now Paul and his companions traveled throughout the region of Phrygia and

Galatia, having been kept by the Holy Spirit from preaching the word in the province of Asia (cf. Acts 16:6). Paul's missionary endeavors "display an extraordinary combination of strategic planning and keen sensitiveness to the guidance of the Spirit of God, however that guidance was conveyed—by prophetic utterance, inward prompting, or the overruling of external circumstances."[7]

"When they came to the border of Mysia, they tried to enter Bithynia, but the Spirit of Jesus would not allow them in. So they passed by Mysia and went down to Troas." Their attempt to penetrate Bithynia would seem a natural extension of their ministry, allowing for no creative alternative. At Troas, a series of prohibitions would give way to positive direction.

Paul had a vision during the night concerning a man of Macedonia, standing and begging him: "Come over to Macedonia and help us." Accordingly, "*we* got ready at once to leave for Macedonia, concluding that God had called *us* to preach the gospel to them." This seemed to be a natural inference, that did not require extended reflection. However, it solicited a corporate response.

This, in turn, brings to mind the sage observation: "For lack of guidance a nation falls, but many advisers make victory sure" (Prov. 11:4). A person is well-advised to seek the input of others, even when it comes to creative innovation. Of course, it goes without saying that we should select our mentors carefully.

Still, certain persons cultivate their creative potential more than others. I recall a former colleague who left the teaching profession for what he described as *pure research*. While observing certain parameters, he was free to explore whatever seemed inviting, It was supposed that this would at some point lead to profitable application.

Another friend turned his creative imagination into improving the operation of the plant in which he worked. With clip-board in hand, he walked from one phase of the operation to another—sketching alternative procedures. He assured me that the company payed him generously for his insightful input.

Then, finally, "Must then Christ perish in torment in every age to save those that have no imagination?"[8] So it is with this provocative inquiry that we conclude the initial segment of the mystery and meaning of Holy Writ.

PART TWO

PART TWO

15

ALL SCRIPTURE

"All Scripture is God-breathed (inspired) and is useful for teaching, rebuking, correcting and training in righteousness, so that the man of God may be thoroughly equipped for every good work" (2 Tim. 3:16). In keeping with this thesis, "you must understand that no prophecy of Scripture came about by the prophet's own interpretation. For prophecy never had its origin in the will of man, but men spoke from God as they were carried along with the Holy Spirit" (2 Peter 1:20-21).

This does not rule out the human factor, but quite the reverse. More expressly, the writers were *carried along* by way of the Spirit—in a manner that highlights their individual differences. Then, too, so as to accommodate divine truth.

This realization has wide-ranging implications for how we interpret Holy Writ. For instance, Justin Martyr observes: "since I am entirely convinced that no Scripture contradicts another, I shall admit rather that I do not understand what is recorded, and shall strive to persuade those who imagine that the Scriptures are contradictory to be rather of the same opinion as myself."[1] Thus assured, he sets out to discover how the text complements itself.

Marcion provides a study in contrast. He held that the Old Testament was written by a lesser deity. Not content with this disclaimer, he purged the New Testament of all that did not appeal to him. His truncated cannon of Scripture incited the early church to set forth an alternative more in keeping with what was commonly accepted.

"This is what I told you while I was still with you," Jesus reminded his disciples: "Everything must be fulfilled that is written about me in the Law of Moses, the Prophets and the Psalms" (Luke 14:44).

All three parts of the OT are referred to: **the Law of Moses, the Prophets, and the Psalms**. The Psalms should be understood as referring to the third division of the

Hebrew Bible usually known as the 'Writings' . . . probably because of all the
Writings, the Psalms yielded the greatest relevance for a christological interpretation of the OT.[2]

Furthermore, Peter allows that Paul's "letters contain some things that are hard
to understand, which ignorant and unstable people distort, as they do the other
Scriptures, to their own destruction" (2 Peter 3:16). This would seem to acknowledge a growing body of literature, deserving of the designation *Scripture*. In
particular, that associated with the apostolic tradition.[3]

That is to say, each book had to be written either by an apostle or by one
associated with an apostle. In this regard, Eusebius recalls "Mark, to whom the
Gospel is ascribed, as being the companion of Peter, that he would leave in writing
a record of the teaching which had been delivered to them verbally."[4] Luke,
moreover, was a companion of the apostle Paul.

Should, however, the apostolic connection be suspect, the book would not have
ready acceptance. Such was the case with Hebrews, which some attributed to Paul
while others were undecided. This might suggest that it was written by one of the
apostle's associates, especially in light of its inclusion in the cannon.

How are we to understand the deference given to the apostles? According to the
Talmud, "The one who is sent is as the one who sends." So it was that Jesus summoned twelve of his disciples, and designated them apostles (cf. Matt. 10:1-2). It
came to pass that they presided over the fledgling community, and sought to ground
them in the faith.

In response, the believers "devoted themselves to the apostle's teaching and to
the fellowship" (Acts 2:42). This, for all practical purposes, came to be embodied
in the New Testament texts. Accordingly, Origin asserts: "It appears to me that one
who is able to represent in a genuine manner the doctrine of the Church . . . should
take his stand against historical fictions, and oppose them (with the) lofty evangeical
message found both in the so-called Old Testament and the so-called New."[5]

If inspired of God, it should come as no surprise that it *is useful for teaching,
rebuking, and correcting and training in righteousness. Teaching* and *correcting*
are set over against each other, corresponding to positive and negative reenforce-
ment. *Teaching* and *correcting* reverses the order, while retaining the contrast.

The man of God likely pertains to one who assumes a leadership role in the faith
community. These needed to exercise special care to fine-tune their ministry to the
teachings of Holy Writ. This is in keeping with Jesus' dictum: "From everyone who
has been given much, much will be demanded, and from the one who has been
entrusted with much, much more will be asked" (Luke 12:48).

The text could apply in an extended sense to others. If for no other reason than
church leaders are meant to live exemplary lives. Consequently, the ultimate purpose for interpreting Scripture is not simply to know, but to do. This is a thesis we
shall explore in greater length at a later point.

For now, note that the person should be thoroughly equipped *for every good
work*. It brings to mind the long hours of practice needed to excel in an athletic
sport. Day in and day out, whenever the opportunity affords itself. Then, in antic-

ipation of when it will be necessary to call on every reserve so as to succeed.

"What are *mitzvot* (sing. *mitzvah*)? The word is usually translated as 'command-ment,' but it also has come to mean 'good deed' colloquially. But good deed misses the core of the concept by a long way."[6] Mainly because it overlooks the religious dimension of the injunction.

These consist of positive and negative mandates. In Jewish tradition, *belief in God* heads the list of positive demands. All that is good and wholesome is said to derive from a vibrant faith. In this regard, the Westminster Confession identifies the chief end of man is to glorify God and enjoy him forever.

Conversely, *not believing in any other God* heads the list of negative injunc-tions. All evil is said to evolve from idolatry. The Decalogue is adamant at this point, "You shall have no other gods before me" (Exod. 20:3). Not in the sense of priority, but as if to worship another in God's presence.

The *mitzvot* extend into many related areas. For instance, to embrace *the love of God*. "Teacher," a scribe inquired of Jesus, "which is the greatest commandment in the Law?" (Matt. 22:36).

Jesus pointedly replied, "Love the Lord your God with all your heart and with all your soul and with all your mind. . . . And the second is like it: Love your neighbor as yourself. All the Law and Prophets hang on these two commandments." He thus draws together two crucial texts (cf. Deut. 6:5 and Lev. 19:18) so as to demonstrate their relatedness. Along this line, "For anyone who does not love his brother, whom he has seen, cannot love God, whom he has not seen" (1 John 4:20).

Love God without equivocation and one's neighbor as oneself, and all the rest appears as commentary. Jesus thereby provides an invaluable key to the interpretive process. So that it provides a means for us to get our bearings when confused by the many cross-currents revealed in the text.

Fearing God is listed next in Jewish reckoning. The accent is on due reverence, and is extended to others to whom honor is due (cf. Rom. 13:7). This is as evi-denced both by what we say and do.

Some of the commandments are more concrete. As an example, *paying wages on time*. This could be a critical concern if the laborers were struggling to get by. In any case, the failure to be prompt in paying was considered a form of steal-ing—as was slander.

Honoring one's parents was yet another highly acclaimed *mitzvah*. This was to be embraced through heeding their counsel, treating them with respect, and seeing that their needs were met. Then, once they had passed away remembering them in appropriate ways—such as recalling cherished times together.

The negative commandments also cover a large range of topics. For instance, *do not marry a heretic*. Since this would likely compromise one's faith, and endanger the children born of the union. Accordingly, one was not supposed to assume that marriage would necessarily correct the way of an erring partner.

Neither was one *to partake of any unclean creature*. Such as was delineated in the covenant. In one instance, apparently for health reasons. In another, because they were associated with pagan practices. And again, perhaps simply to heighten the identity of a chosen people. The Jerusalem Council serves as a prime example of how this issue was resolved within the Christian community (cf. Acts 15).

Then, too, *not to put another to shame*. Such as when we presume to know another person's intent, and castigate him for that reason. Conversely, for failing to correct an individual, thus allowing him or her to fall into disrepute. So also through a general lack of civility in our conversation with others.

As a final case in point, *not to be promiscuous*. Through sexual intercourse with persons other than one's spouse, or otherwise violating the marriage ideal. Which, in turn, recalls the account of *a bleeding nose Pharisee*, who closed his eyes so not to lust after an attractive women, and thus collided with a wall. He was ridiculed for manifest legalism, while contrasted to those who resembled the patriarch Abraham—pointedly declared to be a friend of God.

The above line of reasoning assumes an emerging rabbinic tradition, extant at the time of Paul and relevant for our understanding of his appeal. While this could be documented, it would unnecessarily encumber our present discussion. It is suffice to bear in mind Paul's rabbinic credentials, "Under Gamaliel I was thoroughly trained in the law of our fathers" (Acts 22:3).

Qualifications aside, we are thus assured that the inspiration of Scripture should be taken as a guarantee of consistency among its various components. Accordingly, God does not say one thing on a certain occasion, only to contradict himself on another.

Conversely, its human character is not thereby compromised. We are assured of this by Paul's rabbinic reasoning in the foregoing discussion. It can be illustrated time and again throughout Holy Writ. Consequently, it is well to bear in mind that Scripture reports to be God's word in human expression.

16

SALVATION HISTORY

The notion of *salvation history* was bequeathed to us by J. C. K. von Hoffmann and the Erlangen School, a conservative wing of nineteenth century Lutheran thought. It stressed the importance of viewing Scripture in its entirety, as an expression of God's redemptive activity. Even so, it was elaborated in three diverse contexts. First, with emphasis on the factual events whereby God achieves his gracious purposes. Second, concerning the personal appropriation of divine initiatives. Finally, regarding the proclamation of these events as a key to understanding the text.

We will proceed in narrative fashion, with broad brush strokes, and select commentary. Moses had fled into the region of Midian, where he was tending his father-in-law's flock, and saw a burning bush that was not consumed. At this, he turned aside to view this strange phenomenon more closely. Whereupon, a voice called to him from out of the bush (cf. Exod. 3:4).

"Do not come any closer," the voice cautioned him. "Take off your sandals, for the place where you are standing is holy ground." After that, it continued: "I am the God of your father, the God of Abraham, the God of Isaac and the God of Jacob." Moses hid his face, because he was afraid to confront the Almighty.

"I have indeed seen the misery of my people in Egypt," God informed him. "So now, go. I am sending you to Pharaoh to bring my people the Israelites out of Egypt." Moses did not feel up to the challenge. "I will be with you," God assured him.

Moses was still reluctant to undertake so problematic a task. "Suppose I go to the Israelites and say to them, 'The God of your fathers has sent me to you,' and they ask me, 'What is his name?' Then what shall I tell them?" "Normally, in patriarchal days, any new revelation of the ancestral God will be summed up in a new title for Him (Gen. 16:13) which will in the future both record and recount a deeper knowledge of God's saving activity."[1]

God replied, "I AM WHO I AM. This is what you are to say to the Israelites: I AM has sent me to you." He was thus revealed as the *living God*; and by implication, one capable of fulfilling his promises.

We break away from the narrative at this point so as to pick it up again with Moses' return to Egypt. There he was greeted by Aaron. Afterward, they went before Pharaoh and said: "This is what the Lord, the God of Israel says: 'Let my people go, so that they may hold a festival to me in the desert'" (5:1).

The ruler incredulously replied, "Who is the Lord, that I should obey you and let Israel go? I do not know the Lord and I will not let Israel go." That very day he increased the demands made on the oppressed people.

Consequently, the Almighty visited plagues on the land. At this, Pharaoh relented. "Up!" he enjoined Moses and Aaron. "Leave my people, you and the Israelites! Go worship the Lord as you have requested. Take your flocks and herds, as you have said, and go. And also bless me" (12:31-32).

However, Pharoah and his officials subsequently had second thoughts. "What have we done?" they inquired. "We have let the Israelites go and have lost their services!" They quickly assembled a formidable task force, and set out in hot pursuit.

When the Israelites saw the Egyptians approaching their encampment by the sea, they complained to Moses: "Was it because there were no graves in Egypt that you brought us to the desert to die?" (14:11).

"Do not be afraid," Moses assured the people. "Stand firm and you will see the deliverance the Lord will bring you today." Then Moses stretched out his hand, and all night the Lord drove the water back with a strong east wind—so that they were able to negotiate the barrier.

When the Egyptians attempted to pursue them, the Lord prompted Moses: "Stretch out your hand over the seas so that the waters may flow back over the Egyptians and their chariots and horsemen." So it was that the waters engulfed them. "I will sing to the Lord, for he is highly exalted," the people enthused. "The horse and the rider he has hurled into the sea. The Lord is my strength and my song; he has become my salvation" (15:1).

All things considered, we are reminded of the character of salvation history. It begins with an event. Something happened, involving certain persons, revealing God's redemptive activity.

Moreover, the event is appreciatively recalled. "Who among the gods is like you," the people rhetorically inquire, "majestic in holiness, awesome in glory, working wonders?" You and you alone are deserving of praise.

Which, in turn, calls for commitment. "In your unfailing love you will lead the people you have redeemed. In your strength you will guide them to your holy dwelling." Let it be so.

The scene shifts. The good news is that the people, after years of wandering in the wilderness, have made their way into the promised land. The bad news is that they have failed to drive out its inhabitants, eliciting the turbulent time of the judges.

The seemingly inconsequential words "Now it came to pass" (Judges 1:1) conveys an important truth. "They tell us that the ultimate context for the study of the book is the entire panorama which begins with creation, and extends on to Abraham, Moses, Joshua, the Judges, Samuel, David, the kings of Israel, and Jesus Christ."[2] Accordingly, we are assured that salvation history is on course.

We are pointedly reminded from time to time, "In those days Israel had no king; everyone did as he saw fit" (17:6, 18:1, 19:1; 21:25). This created a virtual state of anarchy, soliciting the observation: "Some order is better than none."

"A common cycle occurs throughout the narrative. First, the Israelites do evil in the sight of the Lord. Then, seeing that they could not restrain sin within, they could not contain evil without."[3] Consequently, they were oppressed by others. At this, they cry out to the Lord. In response, he sends them a deliverer. They enjoy peace for a time, before again initiating the predictable pattern.

The scene again shifts. Throughout Samuel's lifetime, the hand of the Lord was on him. When he became advanced in years, he appointed his sons to follow in his stead. However, they did not walk in the ways of the Lord. "They turned aside after dishonest gain and accepted bribes and perverted justice" (1 Sam. 8:3).

So it was that the elders approached Samuel with the request that he appoint a king over them. Saul appeared to be a likely candidate. He came from the small tribe of Benjamin, and would for that reason not constitute so great a threat to invested interests. Then, too, he was "an impressive young man without equal among the Israelites—a head taller than any of the others" (9:2), and appealingly humble (9:21; 10:22).

Power tends to corrupt, and Saul proved to be no exception. Things turned from bad to worse. He offered a sacrifice when Samuel was delayed, took plunder and rationalized his behavior, attempted to slay David, killed the priests of Nob, and violated the prohibition against contacting mediums. The days of his reign were numbered.

In contrast to Saul's dismal failure, David's reign appeared even more spectacular. He would become the paradigm by which all subsequent rulers are measured. As an example, God remonstrated with Jeroboam: "I tore the kingdom away from the house of David and gave it to you, but you have not been like my servant David, who kept my commands and followed me with all his heart, doing only what was right in my eyes" (1 Kings 14:6).

Notwithstanding, David sinned grievously. One evening he arose from his bed, and walked around on the roof of the palace. From there he could see a woman bathing. She was very beautiful. He sent for her, and they slept together.

When she became pregnant, David sent for her husband Uriah, who was away on a military expedition, in hopes that his indiscretion could be kept secret. When this did not succeed, he arranged for Uriah is be slain. Afterward, he wed Bathsheba.

Now the Lord dispatched the prophet Nathan to reprove the monarch. David contritely responded, "I have sinned against the Lord." His last words were in the form of an oracle: "When one rules over men in righteousness, when he rules in the fear of God, he is like the light of morning at sunrise or a cloudless morning, like the brightness after rain that beings the grass from the earth" (23:1).

Solomon ruled in his stead. "Ask for whatever you want me to give you," the Lord encouraged him. In response, the ruler asked for a discerning heart to govern the people. At this, the Lord confided: "Since you have asked for this and not for long life or wealth for yourself, nor have asked for the death of your enemies but for discernment in administering justice, I will do what you have asked." Moreover, he promised the ruler both riches and honor.

Even so, Solomon multiplied his alliances, as indicated by a large and diverse harem. They, in turn, compromised his devotion to the Almighty. All three kings had begun well, but ended tragically. The kingdom was rent in two. The northern kingdom went into a tight spiral, from which there was no recovery. The southern kingdom fared better, enjoying times of covenant renewal. However, it eventually succumbed to its hostile neighbors.

The privileged class was whisked away into captivity, leaving the remainder to manage as best they could. The resulting social disintegration brought to mind the creation account when the world was formless and empty (cf. Jer. 4:23). As for those taken into exile, "By the rivers of Babylon we sat and wept when we remembered Zion. . . . How can we sing the songs of the Lord while in a foreign land?" (Psa. 137:1, 4). The time came when they were allowed to return. It is sometimes referred to as *the new exodus*, picking up on the deliverance theme running through Holy Writ.

Now the school of the prophets was hushed. It seemed as if God had grown tired of admonishing his wayward people. "The silent years were decidedly not uneventful. Philip of Macedon took the initial step toward forming the Hellenic League as a rival to Persia. Murdered in 316 B.C., he was succeeded by his youthful son Alexander."[4]

Hellenism was making substantial inroads into the Jewish community, not necessarily as a result of calculated efforts. "It was simply that Greek thought was in the air and inevitably made its impact on the minds of Jewish thinkers as they grappled with the new problems that their age had raised"[5]

Hellenism played to mixed reviews. Some saw it as a welcomed means of casting off archaic tradition, and accommodating to current situations. Others viewed it as a threat to the very existence of the chosen people. Antiochus IV brought matters to a head. In a dramatic encounter outside Alexandria, he was forced to give up his invasion of Egypt. With dreams of grandeur shattered, and prestige diminished, he took out his frustration on Jerusalem. The drunken orgy associated with the worship of Bacchus was made compulsory. Jews were forbidden, under the penalty of death, to practice circumcision, Sabbath observance, and the annual festivals.

This gave rise to the Maccabean revolt. When coupled with insurrection at home, the Syrians were forced to retreat. The Jews were eventually freed from taxation, thought tantamount to independence. Nevertheless, the idealism of the Maccabees was in decline. The Romans intervened, and as cogently expressed by Josephus: "Judea was made tributary to the Romans." So the stage was set for what would subsequently be set forth in the gospels.

It came to pass that God sent the angel Gabriel to Nazareth, to a virgin pledged to marry Joseph of the lineage of David. She was named *Mary*. "Greetings, you who are highly favored!" the angel exclaimed. "The Lord is with you" (Luke 1:28).

Mary was greatly troubled at his words, not knowing what to make of them. "Do not be afraid," he assured here. "Mary, you have found favor with God. You will be with child and give birth to a son, and you are to give him the name Jesus." Now *Jesus* was not an uncommon name. Even so, its meaning—God is my Savior—was most applicable for Jesus of Nazareth.

Caesar Augustus subsequently issued a decree that a census should be taken throughout the empire. Accordingly, Joseph and Mary made their way to Bethlehem, since (as noted above) he was of the house of David. There Mary gave birth to a son, whom she wrapped in cloths and laid him in a manger. This was likely adjacent to the private living quarters of a family, and perhaps relatives.

There were shepherds living out in the fields nearby, keeping watch over their flocks at night. An angel of the Lord appeared to them, and the glory of the Lord shone round about them—causing them to be terrified. "Do not be afraid," the angel assured them. "I bring you good news of great joy that will be for all the people. Today in the town of David a Savior has been born to you; he is Christ the Lord" (2:10-11).

The shepherds were likely non-observant Jews, characterized as *sinners* in the gospel accounts. Consequently, their selection as recipients of the good news prefigured the proclamation of the gospel to all people. This, in turn, would be in keeping with the theme Luke carefully develops through his two-volume work: Luke/Acts.

Suddenly a great company of the heavenly host appeared with the angel, praising God and saying: "Glory to God in the highest, and on earth peace to men on whom his favor rests." When the angels had left them, the shepherds set out to verify what was told them. Having done so, they returned—glorifying and praising God.

Jesus was about thirty years of age when he began his public ministry (cf. 2:23). This would be along the line of the requirement for service in the Tent of Meeting (cf. Num. 4:3). In more general terms, it signaled that the person had reached a time of mature judgement.

One incident will serve to illustrate the redemptive character of Jesus' public ministry. He and his disciples came to a town in Samaria called *Sychar*. Jacob's well was there, and Jesus—being weary from the journey, sat down by the well. When a Samaritan woman came to draw water, Jesus inquired of her: "Will you give me a drink?" (John 4:7).

"You are a Jew and I am a Samaritan women," she protested. "How can you ask me for a drink?" "For Jews do not associate with Samaritans," John editorializes.

Jesus replied, "If you knew the gift of God and who it is that asks you for a drink you would have asked him and he would have given you living water."

"Sir," the woman objected, "You have nothing to draw with and the well is deep. Where can you get this living water."

Jesus answered, "Everyone who drinks this water will be thirsty again, but whoever drinks the water I give him will never thirst. Indeed, the water I give him will become in him a spring of water welling up to eternal life." As if to confirm his words, the woman and many of those in the village came to put their faith in him.

Jesus' public ministry would be short-lived. He "began to explain to his disciples that he must go to Jerusalem and suffer many things at the hands of the elders, chief priests and teachers of the law, and that he must be killed and on the third day be raised to life" (Matt. 16:21).

This was in accord with God's redemptive strategy. In retrospect, "God demonstrates his own love for us in this: While we were still sinners, Christ died for us" (Rom. 5:8). In terms of the haunting lyric, this constituted *amazing grace.*

Once Jesus was raised from the dead, he mandated that his disciples wait in Jerusalem until they were endued with power from on high. So it came to pass that on the day of Pentecost the Holy Spirit was poured out on those assembled. This was to enable them to disciple all nations (cf. Acts 1:8).

Accordingly, the fledgling community fearlessly proclaimed the good news. Not uncommonly it was at great personal cost. There were many martyrs, soliciting Tertullian's often repeated rejoinder: "The oftener we are mown down by you, the more in number we grow; the blood of Christians is seed."[6]

The Christians were energized by their hope in the blessed return of the Lord in glory. In this regard, "For the Lord himself will come down from heaven, with a loud command, with the voice of the archangel and with the trumpet of God. After that, we will be caught up to meet the Lord. And so we will be with the Lord forver" (1 Thess. 4:16-17).

This would eventuate in God's consummate rule, when the resistive forces of evil are overcome. *Shalom* (peace, well-being) will eventuate. Or, as I like to characterize it, the trains will run on time.

Given this perspective, H. Edmonds confides:

Enough that Jesus saves, this ends my fear and doubt;
a sinful soul, I came to him, he'll never cast me out.
I need no other argument, I need no other plea,
it is enough that Jesus died, and that he died for me.

Thus salvation history concludes on a triumphant note.

17

FUSION OF HORIZONS

Scripture introduces us to a culture far removed from our own by time and orientation. There are strange practices, seemingly without current equivalency. There are unusual expressions, once common place but no longer. There is often a lack of precision, taken for granted in today's world.

This problematic concern is addressed in *philosophic hermeneutics*. It constitutes an effort to discover how an ancient text remains relevant for today. Accordingly, it results in a new challenge for each generation. While an exceedingly complex issue, we can hope only to scratch the surface on this occasion.

Friedrich Schleiermacher is said to have transformed hermenuetics from a literary exercise to a philosophic discipline. While there were more modest precedents, the claim is not far off target. For better and worse, we trace the task from this juncture.

His notes on hermeneutics date from 1805 to 1833. He was fighting a battle on two fronts: with the erudite disposers of religion on the one hand and religious dogmatists on the other. The Enlightenment had encouraged persons to throw off religious constraints, and exercise autonomous reason in their pursuit of truth. .

Schleiermarcher reasoned that religious experience constituted *the consciousness of absolute dependence*. He thus hoped to escape from the theological controversies rampant at the time, and thus commend religion to thoughtful persons. Moreover, he insisted that dogma was no guarantee of religious piety, and could be a hindrance.

As a result, he accented the critical role of the interpreter. This was memorably expressed in the assertion, "One must understand as well and better than the author"[1] *As well*, since he supposed that no one has a privileged access to truth; *and better*, because matters might appear clearer in retrospect. Qualifications aside, in that he gave deference to general revelation over against special revelation.

Even so, he allowed that the text provides the parameters for understanding, so that we cannot simply interpret Scripture any way we wish. It remains for religious experience to endow the text with universal significance. "These two sides of interpretation cannot always coincide," he readily admitted. "For that would presuppose both a complete knowledge of and completely correct use of the language. The 'art' lies in knowing when one side should give way to the other."[2]

Karl Barth would a century later pronounce the whole effort ill-conceived, even though others (like Wilhelm Dilthey) attempted to salvage the endeavor. In particular, Barth concluded that his predecessor had compromised the integrity of the biblical text.

Hans-Georg Gadamer subsequently suggested that the interpretive process resembles the fusion of two horizons. Anthony Thisleton appreciatively comments:

> The nature of the hermeneutical problem is shaped by the fact that both the text and the interpreter are conditioned by their given place in history. For understanding to take place, two sets of variables must be brought into relation with each other. Gadamer's image of the fusion of horizons offers one possible way of describing the main problem and task of hermeneutics.[3]

Gadamer, moreover, speaks for himself: "Every encounter with tradition that takes place within historical consciousness involves the experience of the tension between the text and the present."[4] Since we cannot assimilate the truth readily, we must retain a measure of tentativeness that respects the integrity of both the text and interpreter. "In fact the horizon of the present is being continually formed," Gadamer continues. "An important part of this testing is the encounter with the past and the understanding of tradition from which we come. Hence, the horizons of the present cannot be formed without the past."

The process of testing (fusion) is hence ongoing. The interpreter has no vantage point outside tradition from which to construct religious universals. Schleiermacher was as culture-bound as any other, and perhaps more than most—since he seems not to have been sufficiently aware of his limitations.

It remained for Krister Stendahl to emphasize the discontinuity between the past and present. "There can be little doubt that in the realm of intellectual history, and by implication far beyond it, the realistic biblical interpreters were vastly superior to their predecessors," he cogently concludes. "In its purest scientific form this historical realism is utterly indifferent to our needs and our questions. It is even consciously suspicious of them, since they threaten to lead to anachronistic distinctions."[5]

Consequently, he calls for a calculated detachment in our approach to interpretation. This is quite apart from the quest for relevance. Our concern should be with what the text says, rather than what it says to me or us.

"It can be rightly maintained that liberal theology has often shown itself incapable of descriptive historical research," Stendahl additionally protests. "The principles of interpretation allowed and even required the materials to be arranged so that the texts were not given a chance to speak their original language. The application for our own time was built right into the exegesis itself."[6]

Several propositions can now be set forth, in an attempt to further clarify the issue. First, it is no easy task to interpret Scripture from a context far removed in time and cultural milieu. It demands that we refine our interpretive tools in a conscientious and devout manner. We should be willing to recognize wherein we have erred, and ready to make good use of the insights we have gained.

Second, some have chosen to address this problem from the perspective of the interpreter, while others in terms of the historical and literary character of the text. While both are legitimate concerns, one must not be allowed to override the other.

Third, the text deserves special consideration, since it—rather than our application—constitutes God's inspired word. In particular, we ought not to contradict the evident teaching of Holy Writ. Nor should we pontificate when it comes to our problematic projections. Qualifications aside, speak where the Scripture is clear, and refrain otherwise.

Fourth, the *fusion of horizons* has appealed to many as a realistic construct for hermeneutics. Even so, a distinction must be made. In particular, the far horizon (scripture) remains fixed, while the near horizon (culture) is constantly changing. In other words, we appropriate the former in order to apply it to the latter.

Finally, the interpretive task is passed on from one generation to the next. This results in part from interim discoveries that provide insight into the text. Then, too, we can refine our procedures, so as to minimize the margin of error.

It remains to illustrate how complex and challenging the task may become. If, for instance, we suppose that the Genesis account was written from the context of the exodus, it appears as an emancipation proclamation. Man was born free, and meant to live free. In keeping with this thesis, Jewish tradition portrays the bondage in Egypt as the seventh and climactic rebellion of man against God's righteous counsel.

"True freedom and redemption, in the Jewish view, involve both spiritual and physical liberation."[7] For this reason, Jews were admonished that no one is genuinely free so long as anyone remains in captivity. Israelites who voluntarily embraced slavery were meant to be released the next jubilee year. Gentile slaves were not guaranteed release, although manumission was practiced. Then, too, slaves were to be treated humanely. As a matter of record, they not uncommonly fared better than subsistence laborers.

The undesirability of slavery can be illustrated in various ways. For instance, Paul affirms in his defense before Agrippa that he wished all persons were as he except *for these chains* (cf. Acts 26:29). Moreover, he reflects concerning the runaway slave Onesimus: "Perhaps the reason he was separated from you for a little while was that you might have him back for good—no longer as a slave but better than a slave, as a dear brother" (Philem. 13).

"Were you a slave when you were called?" Paul inquires on another occasion. "Don't let it trouble you—although if you can gain your freedom, do so" (1 Cor. 7:21). This would seem the practical application of what we have considered.

In many instances, Christians took it upon themselves to free their slaves. So also to provide for them during the difficult time of transition. This sometimes required considerable courage, especially when the practice was officially discouraged. Chrysostom, for instance, reasoned that since in Christ there is neither bond nor free, manumission should be practiced (cf. Gal. 3:28).

Slavery in Europe had virtually come to an end by the fourteenth century. However, many Christians owned slaves during the interim. The practice was defended by such prominent third century advocates as Clement of Alexandria and Origin.

Upon being revived in the seventeenth century, it drew the ire of William Wilberforce—as a prominent example. Two years before he relinquished his seat in the House of Commons, he petitioned his associates to abolish slavery. A few days before he passed away, he received word that Parliament had passed the Abolition Act.

Even after slavery had run its course in the British Empire, it continued unabated in adjacent areas—most notably the United States, Brazil, and Mexico. From 1502 to the 1860s, it is estimated that about forty-seven percent were located in Spanish colonies, forty-one percent in Brazil, and a relatively small seven percent in the United States.

Harriet Beecher Stowe's *Uncle Tom's Cabin* helped to bring the plight of the slaves before the American populace. It cast Uncle Tom in the role of a suffering servant, afflicted by his slave master. He refuses to take revenge, in spite of the urging of his fellow slaves, and continues to trust the promises of Christ to sustain him in adversity.

This, in turn, recalls the crucial role the Christian faith played in the life of the oppressed. In this regard, "The Negro church was virtually the only place where slaves were allowed to congregate, to experience a spiritual union with other slaves, and to feel equal to the white man, especially in the eyes of God."[8]

Slavery was eventually abolished as an American institution. Yet, not without considerable sacrifice and suffering. Even so, its effects still linger—creating social tensions and mistrust. All things considered, we are reminded that the task of applying abiding truths to current situations is not simply an academic exercise, but a critical component for social engagement.

18

LITERARY GENRE

The reconciliation of divine transcendence and immanence remains the most critical theological issue that confronts us. This is borne out in the range of literary genre accommodated by Scripture. While discussed in an earlier context, we will explore the topic more fully on this occasion.

WISDOM LITERATURE

"Just as the artisan forges his sword or weaves a rug, so the sage tells us how to live life with finesse. He corrects those of us who blunder along, from one day to the next, saying the wrong thing, doing the wrong thing, wishing we could do better."[1] Welcome to wisdom literature.

"The fear of the Lord is the beginning of knowledge, but fools despise wisdom and discipline" (Prov. 1:7). Initially, *wisdom* and *folly* are contrasted. As for the former, the wise person embraces instruction; with understanding, gains insight; with insight, skill in living; with skill, the ability to plan ahead; with all, to orient life toward God and in accordance with his will. As for the latter, the fool resists instruction; otherwise expressed, is obstinate; as the saying goes: "resembles an accident waiting to happen; as such is a menace to himself and others.

There are other role players, as noted earlier. The *scoffer* contrasts to the wise and is coupled with the fool, as not only disliking correction but holding the truth up to ridicule.

The *sluggard* is disinclined to engage in worthwhile activity. Should he do so, he is not likely to see it through to a successful conclusion. He, moreover, is reluctant to face up to issues, and is characterized from time to time as being rest-less, helpless, useless, and exasperating.

A *good friend* is constant in his or her devotion (cf. Prov. 17:17). Accordingly, one is candid, accepting, reassuring, and tactful

The *simple person* is uninformed. As such, he or she may be influenced for good or evil. The longer one procrastinates, the more likely that evil will triumph.

The quest for wisdom begins with reverence of God. Expressly, not only that he exists, but is worthy of honor. Leave God out, and life rapidly degenerates.

In greater detail, "Listen, my son, to your father's instruction and do not forsake your mother's teaching" (Prov. 1:8). For this is God's way of passing on a spiritual legacy from one generation to the next. In this manner, we learn to cope with authority in the context of those who genuinely care for us.

"The memory of the righteous will be a blessing, but the name of the wicked will not" (10:7). Blessing and shame alike live on after we have passed away.

"When words are many sin is not absent, but he who holds his tongue is wise" (Prov. 10:19). In this connection, "Simply being able to repeat a large number of proverbs does not make one wise. A shrewd observer can make almost any proverb into a 'true' statement by using it to comment upon the right occasion."[2]

"There is a time for everything, and a season for every activity under heaven" (Eccles. 3:1). There is a time to be born and a time to die; a time to weep and a time to laugh; a time to be silent and a time to speak. The genuinely wise person is cognizant of the time, and responds appropriately.

Jesus assumed the role of a sage. Accordingly, we observe his "work of healing, why he spoke in aphorisms and parables and beatitudes, why he gathered disciples, why his message had a more universal flavor to it."[3]

As an example, "No one tears a patch from a new garment and sews it on an old one. If he does, he will have torn the new garment, and the patch from the new will not match the old" (Luke 5:36). "Fasting that is eschatologically motivated would be anachronistic, out of time, Jesus declares. The thing for which hope is expressed in fasting is already present."[4]

In conclusion, wisdom literature does not require privileged information. It is readily available to those who are perceptive and good-intentioned. Otherwise, persons compound their problem through neglect.

PROPHETIC LITERATURE

Prophetic literature assumes a conversational mode. "Thus God says" consequently becomes the signature expression of the school of the prophets. It bears repeating, what sort of a person was the prophet? "To us a single act of injustice—cheating in business, exploitation of the poor—is slight; to the prophets, a disaster. To us injustice is injurious to the welfare of the people; to the prophet is a deathblow to existence"[5] He thus reveals a more sensitive awareness of man's defection from God's righteous ways.

Still again, what sort of person was the prophet? "The prophet is human, yet he employs notes one octave too high for our ears. He experiences moments that defy our understanding. Often his words begin to burn where conscience ends."[6] As a result, it was his unenviable task to fine-tune the monarchy to its covenant obligations.

In the prophet's own words, "the year that King Uzziah died, I saw the Lord seated on a throne, high and exalted, and the train of his robe filled the temple" (Isa. 6:1). He was thus assured of God's sovereign control over human affairs, as a prelude to his call. "Above him were seraphs, each with six wings. And they were calling to one another: 'Holy, holy, holy is the Lord Almighty; the whole earth is full of his glory.'" At the sound of their voices, the doorposts and thresholds shook and the temple was filled with smoke. It was an awesome encounter.

"Woe it me!" Isaiah cried out. "I am ruined! For I am a man of unclean lips, and I live among a people of unclean lips, and my eyes have see the King, the Lord Almighty."

"Then one of the seraphs flew to me with a live coal in his hand, which he had taken with tongs from the altar. With it he touched my mouth and said, 'See, this has touched your lips; your guilt is taken away and your sin atoned for.'" Initially, he is purged of his sin. This, in turn, transforms him into a suitable instrument for heralding God's word to others.

Then he heard the voice of the Lord inquiring, "Whom shall I send? And who will go for us?" The Lord seeks those who willingly serve as his emissaries.

At this, Isaiah heartily responded: "Here am I. Send me!" This comes as a fitting response to the events which preceded it. Isaiah is thus poised to carry out the ministry God envisioned for him. Even though he was as yet unaware of all this might imply, or the cost involved.

"Go and tell this people," God admonished him. "'Be ever hearing, but never understanding; be ever seeing, but never perceiving." This served to call attention to their calloused condition.

"For how long, O Lord?" he inquired.

"Until the cities be ruined and without inhabitants," the Lord replied. In anticipation of their being carried away into captivity.

Another time, and concerning a different prophet. "See, I will send you the prophet Elijah before the great and dreadful day of the Lord comes. He will turn the hearts of the fathers to their children, and the hearts of the children to their fathers; or else I will come and strike the land with a curse" (Mal. 4:5-6).

The choice of Elijah to typify the coming prophet may have been suggested by the mention of Horeb, for (like Moses) he received a revelation of God there (cf. 1 Kings 19:8-18). Then again he served as a moral catalyst for spiritual renewal.

> The future ministry of the coming prophet is described in terms of bridging the generation gap. The fifth commandment implied that the home was essentially the school of the community. There authority and trust could be learned as nowhere else and, with the word of God as guide in the home, society could be changed.[7]

The dismal alternative was that the people would harvest what they had sown. Josephus appreciatively recalls John as "a good man, (who) commanded the Jews to exercise virtue, both as to righteousness towards one another, and piety toward God."[8]

"Do not think that I have come to abolish the Law or the Prophets," Jesus solemnly declared; "I have not come to abolish them but to fulfill them" (Matt. 5:17). "Among the many nuances suggested, the following are the main options: (a) to accomplish, obey; (b) to bring out the full meaning; (c) to complete, by giving final revelation of God's will to which the Old Testament pointed forward."[9] Likely all the above.

Jesus did not simply declare God's word, but embodied it. It bears repeating, the formula *I AM* meant "where I am, there God is, there God lives and speaks, calls, asks, acts, decides, loves, chooses, forgives, rejects, suffers, and dies. Nothing bolder can be said, or imagined."[10]

We also recall that prophetic literature introduces a degree of obscurity unlike its wisdom counterpart. As such, it resembles what one confides in another. It is out of the best of intention, it should be added.

APOCALYPTIC LITERATURE

Apocalyptic literature differs from prophecy "in that it did not originate with the spoken word. There is no doubt that a major factor in (its) development was the cessation of prophecy and greater concentration on the importance of Torah."[11] This is not suggesting that it was without antecedents.

In more general terms, apocalypse appears elicited by adversity and oppression. At such times, God seems distant and his ways inscrutable. Accordingly, the writer turns to symbolic expression where words fail him.

Initially, Daniel draws our attention. He is depicted as one of the Jewish aristocracy whisked away to Babylon. He comes to epitomize a life of faithfulness, obedience, and prayer. Such as enabled him to withstand the severe temptations of an alien culture, and rise to a place of prominence.

It came to pass that Nebuchadnezzar had disturbing dreams, coupled with the fact that he could not recall the particulars. Whereupon, he summoned the magicians, enchanters, sorcerers and astrologers to recover the contents of his dreams, and interpret their meaning. These assorted experts "worked on the principle that dreams and their sequel followed an empirical law which, given sufficient data, could be established. The dream manuals consist accordingly of historical dreams and the events that follow them, arranged systematically for each reference."[12]

When the assembled group were unable to recover the ruler's lost memory or make any sense out of his experience, he was about to have them put to death. Daniel, however, requested a stay of execution. Then, in turn, God revealed to him the matter.

It seems that the king had seen a large statue, awesome in appearance. Its head was made of pure gold, its chest and arms of silver, its stomach and thighs of bronze, its legs of iron, and its feet partly of iron and partly of baked clay. "You, O king, are the king of kings," Daniel informed the perplexed official. "The God of heaven has given you dominion and power and might and glory. You are the head of gold" (Dan. 2:37).

"After you, another kingdom will rise, inferior to yours. Next, a third kingdom, one of bronze. Finally, there will be a fourth kingdom, strong as iron"—although mixed with clay and thus vulnerable. "In the time of those kings, the God of heaven will set up a kingdom that will never be destroyed, nor will it be left to another people. It will crush all those kingdoms and bring them to an end, but it will itself endure forever."

Now Daniel had a dream concerning four beasts. The first resembled a lion, and had the wings of an eagle. The second looked like a bear. The third appeared as a leopard, with four heads. After that, there was a terrifying creature. It had large iron teeth, with which it crushed and devoured its victims. Moreover, it had ten protruding horns—calculated to inflict injury.

As Daniel continued to watch, a little horn supplanted three of the prior horns. This horn had eyes like the eyes of a man, and spoke boastfully.

Then "thrones were set in place, and the Ancient of Days took his seat" (7:9). His clothing was white as snow, and his hair white as wool. His throne was flaming with fire, and its wheels were all ablaze. Thousands attended to him and tens of thousands stood before him. His court was convened.

After that,

> there before me was one like a son of man, coming with the clouds of heaven. He approached the Ancient of Days and was let into his presence. He was given authority, glory and sovereign power. His dominion is an everlasting dominion that will not pass away, and his kingdom is one that will never be destroyed.

In spite of the welter of interpretations, there is one thing eminently clear: God will triumph over all his enemies. Then, too, there will be one resembling *a son of man*, who will be instrumental in bringing all this about.

We take our leave at this juncture, so as to reflect in context on Jesus' so-called *little apocalypse*. Now Jesus was walking away from the temple precinct when his disciples called attention to its impressive appearance. "Do you see all these things?" he inquired by way of response. "I tell you the truth, not one stone here will be left on another; every one will be thrown down" (Matt. 24:2).

Then when they had come to the Mount of Olives, they inquired privately of him: "When will this happen, and what will be the sign of your coming and the end of the age?"

> That the two parts of the question are asked in one breath indicates that the disciples could not dissociate the destruction of the temple from the end of the age. The generalizing plural (these things) apparently includes not only the leveling of the temple but events that had to accompany it, such as the fall of the city of Jerusalem.[13]

Jesus' response deliberately distinguishes between the two events. As for the former, "when you see standing in the holy place the abomination that causes desolation (cf. Dan. 8:13) let those in Judea flee to the mountains." The *abomination* draws upon Antiochus IV's profanation of the temple in 167 B.C. As recalled by Josephus, "the king built an altar (to Zeus) upon God's Altar, he slew swine upon it, and offered as sacrifice neither according to the law, nor the Jewish religious worship in the country."[14]

On that occasion, certain of Jesus' followers are reported to have heeded his warning by fleeing to the Trans-Jordan region. This may have contributed to the animosity felt against them in the Jewish environ, in that they were perceived to have fled the City of the Great King at its hour of dire need.

Shifting focus, Jesus continued: "At that time if anyone says to you, "Look, here is the Christ!' or, 'There is the Christ!' do not believe it. . . . For as lightning that comes from the east is visible even in the west, so will be the coming of the Son of Man."

"Immediately after the distress of those days, the sun will be darkened, and the moon will not give its light; the stars will fall from the sky, and the heavenly bodies will be shaken" (cf. Isa. 1:3, 10; 34:4). Taken at face value, it would seem to be an awesome celestial phenomenon. If in a metaphorical sense, then a momentous social upheaval.

"No one knows about that day or hour, not even the angels in heaven, nor the Son, but only the Father." As for apt commentary,

> History will be full of suffering and evil, including the catastrophy of the fall of Jerusalem, that will seem to herald the eschaton and the coming of the promised one. But the coming of the Son of Man, when it occurs, will be so startling and conspicuous, so glorious and great, that it will need no proclaimers and no interpretation.[15]

Several concluding observations would seem in order. First, as mentioned at the outset, this triad of literary genre reflect various degrees of obscurity. These range from the more obvious, concerning wisdom literature; to the least obvious, with apocalypse. Prophetic literature lies between.

Second, apocalyptic discourse characteristically arises out of times of oppression and persecution. On such occasions, it appears that God is especially distant, and life strikingly precarious. This results in "two distinct ages: the present one that is temporal and evil, and the one to come that is timeless and perfectly righteous. The first is under the control of Satan and the second under the immediate supervision of God."[16]

Third, this does not mean that God has for the time being relinquished his sovereignty. Not for a moment! In the confident words of the apostle Paul, "And we know that in all things God works for the good of those who love him, who have been called according to his purpose" (Rom. 8:28). Thus apocalypse will on occasion provide a glimpse into the heavenly sanctuary, as a means of consolation and assurance.

Fourth, it remains for the faithful to be diligent. To this end, Jesus told a parable concerning ten virgins who took their lamps and went out to meet the bridegroom.

He was a long time in coming, so that they all fell asleep. At midnight the cry rang out: "Here's the bridegroom! Come out to meet him!" (Matt. 25:6).

The virgins awoke, and trimmed their lamps. Those without oil petitioned their companions, "Give us some of your oil; our lamps are going out."

"No," the wise responded, "there may not be enough for both us and you. Instead, go to those who sell oil and buy some for yourselves." But while they were gone, the bridegroom arrived. Then when they attempted to gain entry to the wedding banquet, they were refused. "Therefore keep watch," Jesus cautioned, "because you do not know the day or the hour."

Finally, apocalyptic literature is rich in symbolism. Something stands for something else. For instance, a white horse portends victory. If, as it has been said, "one picture is worth a thousand words," then apocalypse speaks volumes.

19

IN CONTEXT

As aptly stated, "A text without a context is a pretext."However, *context* extends to a variety of related matters—as we shall see in the discussion that follows.

Scripture as context. In general terms, the issue of authority has been approached by way of Scripture, tradition, and reason. *Scripture* consists of the Old and New Testaments. As for the former, the patriarchs, prophets, and writings. As for the latter, the apostolic documents—whether actually composed by the apostles or someone associated with them.

Tradition alludes to the accumulated insights of the Christian fellowship. Such as is passed down from one generation to the next, and refined in the process. It is sometimes made explicit by way of creeds and confessions of faith, and at other times simply implicit in the way people think and behave.

The so-called *two source theory* implied that Scripture and tradition were both to be factored into the interpretive process. Vatican II subtly altered the conventional notion of Scripture *and* tradition to that of Scripture *in* tradition. I take it that this was meant to establish the primacy of Holy Writ, even if in qualified terms. In any case, tradition has merit—if for no other reason than to remind us that the whole church (past and present) should be consulted.

Reason is a shorthand way of expressing conventional wisdom. In other words, what is commonly accepted in a given culture. In this regard, Emil Brunner observed that no culture is so pristine but that it comes under the scathing critique of Holy Writ. Conversely, no culture is so degenerate that it cannot serve as a vehicle for the gospel.

Three related factors need to be kept in mind. First, most cultural components are essentially neutral, and need no alteration. Qualifications aside, they are matters of indifference. Providing, that is, that we do not unnecessarily offend others.

Second, some things are simply not acceptable from a biblical perspective. Such as infanticide, or its near cultural equivalent—abortion for convenience. Then, too, anything that was thought to unnecessarily impinge on the sanctity of life.

Finally, some things should be modified. Such as those that will lend support to the family structure. Then, in turn, have a favorable impact on a wide range of concerns. In these and related ways, we can creatively explore the role of Scripture as an interpretive context.

Scripture in context. Moreover, it is important that we consider Scripture *in* context. Interpret particular texts in the light of the overall thrust of Holy Writ. Explain that which is more ambiguous by what is less so, and not given to novel interpretations.

It all originates with a benevolent deity, bent on sharing with his privileged creatures. Man, however, aspired to something greater, and had to settle for something less. In his fallen condition, God's still loves him.

So life continues, not triumphantly but somehow. We manage the best we can by way of God's grace. Looking to the future, when paradise lost will be regained.

After that, we proceed with more manageable units. Initially, concerning the Pentateuch. These initial books have traditionally been associated with Moses, and God's deliverance of his chosen people from bondage. This, in turn, sets the course for all that follows.

Thereupon, whenever books seem to coalesce in some meaningful way. As when associated with the prophets, the life of Jesus, the outreach of the early church, or sharing some common feature—as with the Major Prophets.

Then in yet smaller units. Individual books, such as Isaiah or Romans. Each is distinctive in itself, and worthy of individual attention.

Meanwhile, observing how various topics are explored. As in 1 Corinthians, when the apostle touches on divisions within the fellowship, church discipline, mariage, and the like. In other words, know where you are at all times, and why you are there.

Interpretation inevitably comes down to syntax. "Verbs and their relationships, nouns and their relationships, and clauses or grouping of words functioning as a unit constitute the basic elements of syntax."[1]

Then there are words in and of themselves. Interpret, as best we can, in the light of their change in usage. Accordingly, be ever diligent and alert to new possibilities.

Context: old & new. Worthy of special attention, the biblical text is divided into the Old and New Testaments. This naturally gives rise to questions concerning the continuity and discontinuity between them. Irenaeus complained concerning Marcion that "he advanced the most daring blasphemy against Him who is proclaimed as God by the law and prophets, declaring Him to be the author of evils, to take delight in war, to be infirm of purpose, and even to be contrary to Himself."[2]

The human dilemma also appears constant between the testaments. In creedal terms, sin consists of any lack of conformity to the will of God. As such, it may be expressed by either what we do or fail to do.

This is not a situation man can resolve on his own. God must take the initiative. The cross thus becomes the focal point of redemptive history. All that was before, anticipates it; and all that follows, recalls it.

Some have likened this to a beachhead on enemy soil. It has been secured, and the final result is not in doubt. The struggle continues unabated, the more so as the consummation approaches. However, this amounts to little more than an act of desperation on the part of the adversary.

While much is made of the distinction between grace and works between the two covenants, this seems to be overdrawn. The covenant is by its very nature an expression of grace, rather than resulting from merit. Even so, the law (teachings) acted as a tutor to bring people to Christ (cf. Gal. 4:1-5). In this connection, it distinguishes between what is right and wrong, and points out our failure.

As a result, we are meant to receive the *full rights of sons*. This implies both associated privileges and responsibilities. Accordingly, "From everyone who has been given much, much will be demanded, and from the one who has been entrusted with much, much more will be asked" (Luke 12:48).

This also resembles the military metaphor *high ground*. More expressly, a place of advantage from which we may wage successful warfare. It is not uncommonly secured at great cost, and requires that we seize the opportunity.

Christ as context. As a prime example, "Luther's biblical interpretation is centered in Christ. To him, Scripture is a testimony to Christ. In those portions of Scripture where he did not find this testimony, he spent little time."[3]

In this regard, "For by him all things were created, things in heaven and in earth, visible and invisible, whether thrones or powers or rulers or authorities; all things were created by him and for him. He is before all things, and in him all things hold together" (Col. 1:16-17). Not only is he the agent of creation, but also its goal.

One can readily see how such a text would provide impetus for treating Christ as the interpretive context. Even though it would seem that it falls something short of a genuinely comprehensive approach to Holy Writ.

Faith as context. "Now faith is being sure of what we hope for and certain of what we do not see," Hebrews alerts us. "This is what the ancients were commended for" (11:1). They thus set a precedent for us as well.

Faith does not resemble the proverbial leap in the dark, but is more along the line of a reasoned conclusion. In personal terms, it emphatically involves trust.

"By faith Abraham, when called to go to a place he would later receive as his inheritance, obeyed and went, even though he did not know where he was going." He left behind familiar surroundings, and the security provided by an extended family. In exchange, he faced an uncertain future—except for the promise that God would provide for his needs.

"By faith Abraham, when God tested him, offered Isaac as a sacrifice. (He) reasoned that God could raise the dead, and figuratively speaking, he did receive Isaac back from death." God having provided a substitute sacrifice, the place came to be identified as *The Lord Will Provide*. Then, too, this incident would be remembered as the prime precedent for Hebrew piety.

"And what more shall I say?" the author rhetorically inquires. "I do not have time to tell about Gideon, Barak, Samson, Jepthah, David, Samuel and the prophets, who through faith conquered kingdoms, administered justice, and gained what was promised. Thus *faith* provides a meaningful context within which to interpret the biblical text.

Hope as context. The history of the universe resembles a cosmic tug of war. On the one side, as a result of the Big Bang, matter is being driven increasingly further apart. On the other, there is the relentless pull of gravity. Should the former prevail, the galaxies will continue to recede from one another, until atrophy sets in. Should the latter prevail, they will come rushing back into a cosmic melting pot.

What are we to make of all this? "The scientific prediction of cosmic futility simply reminds us that a kind of evolutionary optimism is inadequate as a ground of hope. If there really is a true and lasting hope, it can only rest in the eternal being of God himself."[4]

"Now we are children of God, and what we will be has not yet been made known. But we know that when he appears, we shall be like him, for we shall see him as he is. Everyone who has this hope in him purifies himself, just as he is pure" (1 John 3:2-3). It is not surprising, therefore, that Jurgen Moltmann concluded that we are more pulled by the future than driven by the past.

This, in turn, recalls bishop Polycarp's spirited reply to the proconsul: "You threaten me with the fire which burns for an hour, and after a little is extinguished, but are ignorant of the fire of the coming judgment and of eternal punishment, reserved for the ungodly. But why do you tarry? Bring forth what you will."[5] Thus *hope* provides yet another inviting context in which to interpret the sacred scriptures.

Love as context. And now three remain: faith, hope and love. But the greatest of these is love" (1 Cor. 13:13). *Faith* in that it is instrumental to life in Christ, *hope* without which we would despair, and *love* which is said to make the world go around.

Initially, we are reminded of God's compassion for his profligate creatures. "For God so loved the world that he gave his one and only Son, that whoever believes in him shall not perish but have eternal life" (John 3:16).

We are encouraged to love God in return (cf. 1 John 4:19). As would a grateful child respond to a solicitous parent. Through appreciative obedience, no less than sentiment. In a sustained fashion, not given to relapses.

In a manner of speaking, love of God may be said to overflow into our love for others. In this connection, Jesus admonished his disciples: "Love each other as I have loved you. Greater love has no one than this, that he lay down his life for his friends" (John 15:12-13).

"If anyone says, 'I love God,' yet hates his brother, he is a liar," John protests. "For anyone who does not love his brother, whom he has seen, cannot love God, whom he has not seen" (1 John 4:20)" "It follows that if a person is seen not to love his brothers, it is unlikely that he loves God. Indeed, he *cannot* love God, since one part of love for God is love for one's brothers."[6]

Exercise love through attentive listening, sage counsel, and constructive encouragement. Then, too, by addressing a wide range of human needs. Some concern food and shelter, others in cultivating self-esteem and acceptance, and still others associated with one's calling. Do so in a constructive manner; one expressive of genuine concern, and willingness to embrace the cost.

Life as context. "The length of our days is seventy years—or eighty, if we have the strength; yet their span is but trouble and sorrow, for they quickly pass, and we fly away" (Psa. 90:10). This psalm is ascribed to Moses, portrayed as *the man of God.* He is primarily recalled concerning two events: the deliverance of the Israelites from bondage, and the giving of the covenant. He also provided an impetus for the prophetic movement.

The psalm consists of three parts, with a transition between the second and third. The first focuses on God, the second on man, and the third on grace. The transition points out, qualifications aside, that man's troubles are of his own making.

"Lord, you have been our dwelling place throughout all generations. Before the mountains were born or you brought forth the earth and world, from everlasting to everlasting you are God." This appears to echo Moses' blessing, "The eternal God is your refuge, and underneath are the everlasting arms" (Deut. 33:27).

Man, by way of contrast, is manifestly transient. Seventy years is set forth as a natural life span. Eighty in more exceptional instances, but with declining vitality. He resembles in this regard the grass, which appears vibrant for the time being—before withering away under the relentless sun (cf. Isa. 40:6-7).

"May the favor of the Lord our God rest upon us; establish the work of our hand for us," the psalmist concludes. So that life will be blessing, not only for us but others as well. Moreover, as commended by the Almighty.

According to conventional wisdom, each person must play the hand he or she was dealt. Some have more to work with than others. God, conversely, is not unrealistic in his expectations. So it is that *life* provides a provocative context in which to explore the meaning of Holy Writ. Since none of these options are necessarily exclusive, we are encouraged to explore the various alternatives.

20

FINE PRINT

I have heard it said, "The truth is in the fine print." In other words, in the details. I have been selective, so as to introduce a topic that could be expanded at much greater length—but would unnecessarily burden the current project.

METAPHOR & KIN

Metaphor associates one thing with another. Conversely, a *simile* makes the association explicit, by means of such expressions as *like* or *as*. A "parable is often an extended simile. An allegory, on the other hand, is an extended metaphor."[1] These can be considered in conjunction with one another, without unduly laboring their particular distinctives.

"Do not be afraid, little flock" Jesus enjoins his disciples, "for your Father has been pleased to give you the kingdom" (Luke 12:32). He thus compares them to a flock of sheep. This recalls an occasion when, from the top of the Herodian, we viewed a shepherd walking out ahead of the flock, with two guard dogs encouraging the flock to keep pace. The latter is perhaps what the psalmist had in mind when he observed, "Surely goodness and love will follow me all the days of my life" (23:6).

"Go!" Jesus mandated: "I am sending you out like lambs among wolves" (Luke 10:3). As such, they would be defenseless against those hostile to them. Accordingly, they were to exercise deliberate care and confident trust.

If well received, "they are to accept hospitality, comport themselves as exemplary guests, and proclaim the coming of salvation in deed and word. In this way they identify themselves intimately with Jesus' own ministry of healing and proclaiming the kingdom."[2]

The *parable* is a striking aspect of Jesus' teaching. "The kingdom of heaven is like a man who sowed good seed in his field," he observed on one occasion. "But while everyone was sleeping, his enemy came and sowed weeds among the wheat, and went away. When the wheat sprouted and formed heads, then the weeds also appeared" (Matt. 13:24).

At this, the owner's servants inquired: "Sir, didn't you sow good seed in the field? Where then did the weeds come from?"

"An enemy has done this," he replied.

His servants inquired further, "Do you want us to go and pull them up?"

"No," he answered, "because while you are pulling the weeds, you may root up the wheat with them. Let both grow together until the harvest. At that time I will tell the harvesters: 'First collect the weeds and tie them in bundles to be burned; then gather the wheat and bring it into my barn.'" Otherwise, they could readily compound the problem.

Certain principles should be kept in mind in interpreting metaphor and that associated with it. First, one should attempt to identify to whom the words are directed. These are sometimes mentioned outright; and on other occasions, they can be determined from the context.

Second, consider the purpose for which the metaphor is employed. In some instances, it may serve more than a single purpose, such as when Jesus taught his disciples in the presence of the multitude. Then, too, cross-reference the incident, as in the case of the gospel parallels.

Third, note the response of those present. Especially where this involves a mixed audience, such as Pharisees, Sadducees, disciples of John, and the like. This is by way of exploring the finer nuances of the text.

Finally, consider the likely application for the time at which the account is recalled. This requires some acquaintance with the history of the early church, and the circumstances surrounding it. Moreover, it provides a ready means for assessing its continuing relevance.

SYMBOLS & SYMBOLIC ACTION

Even a casual reading of Scripture gives the impression that God is disposed to employ object lessons. For instance, he informed Noah: "I have set my rainbow in the clouds, and it will be a sign of the covenant between me and the earth. Never again will the waters become a flood to destroy all life" (Gen. 9:13, 15). This appears to be a subtle reference to a bow held high overhead, as indicative of the person coming in peace. Hence, it is eminently applicable to the situation.

Man also employs symbols. So it was that Laban and Jacob heaped a pile of stones *as a witness* between them. At this, Laban invoked the Almighty: "May the Lord keep watch between you and me when we are away from each other. If you mistreat my daughters or if you take wives besides my daughters, even though no one is with us, remember that God is witness between you and me" (Gen. 31:49-50).

Jacob was agreeable: "This heap is a witness that I will not go past (it) to harm you and you will not go past (it) to harm me. May the God of Abraham and the God of Nahor, the God of their father, judge between us." Any infraction would thus be perceived as an offense against the Almighty.

Some symbols are conveyed by way of visions. "What do you see?" an angel inquired of Zechariah (4:1).

He answered, "I see a solid gold lampstand with a bowl at the top and seven lights on it, with seven channels to the lights. Also there are two olive trees by it, one on the right of the bowl and the other on the left." The prophet was puzzled by the imagery.

The *lampstand* appears to be a reference to the Hebrew community, which serves as a light to the nations (cf. Isa. 42:6). The two *olive trees* sustain the corporate enterprise. "If the main purpose of the vision may tentatively be stated . . . it is to encourage the two leaders, Joshua and Zerubbabel, with a reminder of God's resources, and to vindicate them in the eyes of the community."[3]

Of course, language itself is symbolic. We employ words to recall past events, and anticipate the future. The words are, in turn, accompanied by various inflections and visual expressions. A shrug of the shoulders, meant to suggest indifference. A toss of the heard in derision. All of which is orchestrated by cultural convention.

Names often take on symbolic significance. So it was that the daughter of Pharaoh called the child she discovered *Moses*, since she "drew him out of the water" (Exod. 2:10). Then, too, Mary gave birth to a son, whom she called *Jesus*—"because he will save his people from their sins" (Matt. 1:21).

Numbers can also function in symbolic manner. Underlying the use of the number *seven* appears to be the fact that God created the heavens and the earth in six days, and rested from his creative activity on the seventh. Hence, it comes to take on the notion of comprehensiveness and perfection.

The number *twelve* emerges with the tribes of Israel. It is thus associated with the people of God, in terms of promise and fulfillment. In keeping with this thesis, Jesus "called his twelve disciples to him and gave them authority to drive out evil spirits and to heal every disease and sickness" (Matt. 19:1).

As with numbers, the symbolic significance of *colors* derive from their associations. "Come!" a *living creature* admonished John (Rev. 6:1). He looked, and there was a rider on a white horse. After that there were riders on red, black, and pale horses. The likely symbolism is as follows:

rider on a white horse: a military conqueror
rider on a red horse: one active in combat
rider on a black horse: indicative of famine
rider on a pale horse: symbolic of sickness, death, and hades

Various metals and jewels may also have symbolic nuances. Gold appears to head the list of precious metals. Consequently, "You welcomed him back with rich blessings and placed a crown of pure gold on his head" (Psa. 21:3).

Another example, "the kingdom of heaven is like a merchant looking for fine pearls. When he found one of great value, he went away and sold everything he had and bought it" (Matt. 13:45-46). In the light of this appraisal, kingdom priorities should head the list.

The prophets were especially noted for their symbolic activity. "Now, son of man, take a clay tablet, put it in front of you and draw the city of Jerusalem on it," Ezekiel was enjoined. "Then lay siege to it. Erect siege works against it, build a ramp up to it, set up camps against it and put battering rams around it" (4:1-2).

After that, "Take an iron pan, place it as an iron wall between you and the city and turn your face toward it. It will be under siege, and you shall besiege it. This will be a sign to the house of Israel." "The word, which really means a griddle for baking, elsewhere occurs in texts relating to Israel's sacrificial worship (Lev. 2:5; 6:21; 7:9; 1 Chron. 23:29). It was probably part of Ezekiel's priestly vocabulary"[4]

"Then lie on your left side and put the sin of the house of Israel upon yourself." In this regard, the prophet acts as a scapegoat (cf. Lev. 16:21-22). He was then to lie on his right side in accordance with the sins of Judah.

Consider one final illustration. Jesus rose from his place at the table, removed his outer clothing, wrapped a towel about him, and began to wash his disciples' feet. "Do you understand what I have done for you?" he rhetorically inquired. "I have set you an example that you should do as I have done for you" (John 13:13, 15). In this manner, he alerted them to the fact that true greatness translates into service. In these and countless other instances, symbolic activity graces the biblical text.

IDIOMS & HYPERBOLE

"An *idiom* is an expression peculiar to one particular language. Each language has different ways of saying things. Idioms reveal thought patterns of the people who speak the language."[5] More expressly, that which can not be readily derived from the words themselves.

"So then," Joseph addressed his brothers, "it was not you who sent me here, but God" (Gen. 45:8). The Hebrew idiom does not mean to imply that they were not implicated, since they were. Instead, it means "not only this but that"—since God had an overriding purpose.

As Moses approached the burning bush, a voice cautioned him: "Do not come any closer. Take off your sandals, for the place where you are standing is holy ground" (Exod. 3:5). As previously observed, there are two plausible origins for the means of expressing reverence: "First, it may be the sign of acceptance of a servant's position, for the slave usually went barefoot. Secondly, it may be a relic of very early days when men laid aside all covering and pretense to approach their God."[6]

Another text, "But because they served them (the people) in the presence of their idols and made the house of Israel fall into sin, therefore I have sworn with uplifted hand that they must bear the consequences of their sin" (Ezek. 44:12). This reflects the practice of raising one's hand when confirming an oath.

Hebrew idiom is also given to hyperbole (exaggeration). "If your eye cause you to sin, gouge it out and throw it away," Jesus admonished. "For it is better for you to lose one part of your body than for your whole body to be thrown into hell" (Matt. 5:29). While none familiar with the culture would have actually done so, there are instances where Gentiles took this advice literally.

IRONY AND SUCH

While *irony* is notoriously difficult to define, it expresses something other than the words actually imply. Such as when a person exclaims, "How generous!" When, in fact he means quite the reverse.

Jonah can be singled out for his ironic behavior. "Go to the great city of Nineveh and preach against it," the Lord enjoined him, "because its wickedness has come up before me" (1:1). Instead, he booked passage for Tarshish, which lay in the opposite direction. Accordingly, one is inclined to inquire in disbelief: "What manner of prophet is this?"

Shifting focus, we turn our attention to Jesus. He "is the only character in the Fourth Gospel who utters irony without being the victim of it," Paul Duke observes. "It is intentional . . . often saying subtly less or more than he ostensibly means. Other characters may attempt verbal irony in this Gospel—his opponents often trade in sarcasm—but their intended cleverness always misfires in view of the Truth."[7]

As an example, Jesus observed: "I have shown you many great miracles from the Father. For which of these do you stone me?" (10:32). It seems ironic that they would stone him for doing good.

Satire can appear in conjunction with irony or separate from it. Its intent is to point out human vice or folly through ridicule or rebuke. Accordingly, "Woe to you, teachers of the law and Pharisees, you hypocrites! You give a tenth of your spices—mint, dill and cummin. But you have neglected the more important matters of the law—justice, mercy and faithfulness" (Matt. 23:23).

After which, Jesus exclaimed: "You blind guides! You strain out a gnat but swallow a camel." As for commentary, "They are blind leaders who filter their wine in order to avoid drinking a ceremonially unclean *gnat* (cf. Lev. 11:41) yet gulp down a *camel*. There is a wordplay in Aramaic between *gnat* and *camel* (the words sound very much alike)."[8]

Humor is more comprehensive than the above. Biblical humor tends to be subtle. For instance, Jacob contracted to marry Rachel—who was the younger of two sisters and very attractive. Having slept with who he supposed was Rachel, he awoke, and "there was Leah"—the older and less attractive (Gen. 30:25).

Sometimes humor is more contrived. "How can you say to your brother, 'Let me take the speck out of your eye,' when all the time there is a plank in your own eye?" Jesus inquired. "You hypocrite, first take the plank out of your own eye, and then you will see clearly to remove the speck from your brother's eye" (Matt. 7:4-5). Such was calculated to amuse his audience, while making its point.

POTPOURRI

The *literal* meaning of Scripture has been subject to considerable controversy, sometimes showing up in unexpected contexts—as with the insistence on the *real* presence of Jesus in the communion elements. The term pertains to its commonly acknowledged use, regardless of analogical application. As an extended example, Jesus enjoins his disciples:

> You are the light of the world. A city on a hill cannot be hidden. Neither do people light a lamp and put it under a bowl. Instead they put it on its stand, and it gives light to everyone in the house. In the same way, let your light shine before men, that they may see your good deeds and praise your Father in heaven (Matt. 5:14-16).

Genealogies play a more significant role in antiquity than today. Thus the *Table of the Nations* provided an important link in the narrative (cf. Gen. 10). As I noted on another occasion, three facets are involved:

> First, the human race is united by virtue of being one family. Second, (it) is separated and dispersed as a result of its defiant effort in seeking to erect the tower of Babel. It has consequently failed in the attempt to usurp God's rightful place at life's center. Third, the nations one and all stand within the divine structure of blessings and cursings set forth in the covenant with Noah.[9]

Moreover, Matthew records "the genealogy of Jesus Christ the son of David, the son of Abraham" (1:1). As touched on earlier, this served to establish the legitimacy of Jesus as the Messiah. In particular, as heir to the Davidic Dynasty, and in keeping with the prior promise given to the patriarch. Genealogies might serve other purposes as well, such as validating those of priestly descent, and passing on inheritance.

Hebrew poetry is something of an enigma to the English reader. While the latter relies on *sound*, the former expresses patterns of *thought*. Some take the form of simple parallelism. For instance, "What is man that you are mindful of him, the son of man that you care for him?" (Psa. 8:4). The idea is thus repeated in somewhat different wording.

Conversely, the two lines may be by way of contrast. As an example, "A gentle answer turns away wrath, but a harsh word stirs up anger" (Prov. 15:1). Or one line may set forth in figurative fashion what the other states in literal manner. Along this line, "As the deer pants for streams of water, so my soul pants for you, O God" (Psa. 42:1). Alternative constructions could readily be cited.

As amply illustrated up to this point, it is also important (whenever possible) to locate the text in its *geographical* and *historical* setting. As for the former, to envisage the location where the account originates. As for the latter, to draw upon secular history as applicable. Then, too, to be sensitive to the course of salvation history—as outlined on a previous occasion.

All things considered, to be alert to the finer nuances of the text. Such as might escape the casual reader, and require more rigorous attention. Furthermore, do not take things for granted, since new insights throw the text into bolder relief. Fine-tune the skills we have obtained, as good stewards of God's gracious endowment. Recognize, moreover, that the interpretive task is never complete.

21

WALK THE WALK

Jesus' admonition to do to others as we would have them do to us (cf. Luke 6:31) is perhaps more distinctive than we have been led to believe. "In Hellenistic discussion of ethics, it was ordinarily contextualized within an ethic of consistency and reciprocity. Within this immediate context, however, this can hardly be the meaning. Others are to be treated lovingly, period, without thought to reciprocating behavior."[1] Nor in other alleged instances genuinely equivalent. In any case, it qualifies as *unconditional love.*

Thus are we reminded that our purpose in faithfully interpreting Holy Writ is not simply to better understand but to put it into practice. In this regard, James asserts: "Show me your faith without deeds, and I will show you my faith by what I do" (2:18). "The demand is impossible to meet. Like a horse that cannot be seen, smelled, touched, or ridden, that eats invisible grass and leaves no mark on the ground, such faith is undemonstrable and suspect."[2]

How, then, are we to read Scripture with ethical intent? In the beginning, God created the heavens and the earth. This alerts us to the fact that he has proprietary rights. As noted earlier, the chief end of man is to glorify God and enjoy him forever.

God resembles in this regard a solicitous parent. According to conventional wisdom, father knows best.

This is calculated to foster trustful obedience. In the memorable lyrics of John Sammis:

When we walk with the Lord in the light of his Word,
what a glory he sheds on our way!
While we do his good will, he abides with us still,
and with all who will trust and obey.

"Now the earth was formless and empty, darkness was over the surface of the deep, and the Spirit of God was hovering over the waters" (Gen. 1:1). "This combination of terms (*tohu* and *bohu*) occurs only here and in Jeremiah 4:23, the former with reference to nature and the latter extended to incorporate the disintegration of the social order following the Babylonian invasion."[3]

Thus *chaos* appears a retrogression from the constructive orderliness that God introduced into creation. This occurs as a result of man's lingering resistence to his gracious intent. Not only is man reluctant to let God be God, but fails to assume his comparable responsibilities.

This can be overcome only by means of God's invigorating grace. As has been said, expect great things from God and also undertake great things in his name. Do not settle for less.

So much for the larger picture; we turn now to some of the related particulars. Prayer and the study of Scripture are complementary components of a devotional life. "Prayer is the wall of faith," Tertullian graphically observes: "her arms (armor) and missiles against the foe who keep watch over us on all sides. And so never walk we unarmed."[4] Of similar intent, "The prayer of a righteous man is powerful and effective." (James 5:16).

Even so, prayer is no substitute for the study of Scripture, or the reverse. Instead, they resemble faithful companions. In this regard, they persist in spite of opposition and discouragement.

This brings us to the related matter of divine guidance. It as a rule results from a heightened awareness of God's will as revealed in Holy Writ. This may be coupled with sage counsel, providential timing, and/or fortuitous circumstances.

First, it consists of general principles, such as compassion for others. By way of extension, "Without attention, no meaningful interaction is possible. Our first responsibility, when we are with others, is to pay attention. Only as we *notice* the world can we begin to *care* for it."[5]

Then, too, by being of help. Jesus faulted those who "tie up heavy loads and put them on men's shoulders, but they themselves are not willing to lift a finger to move them" (Matt. 23:4). In contrast, he admonished: "Take my yoke upon you and learn from me, for I am gentle and humble of heart, and you will find rest for your soul" (Matt. 11:28).

Second, it may involve more concrete instructions. As an example, "If your brother sins against you, go and show him his fault, just between the two of you (some manuscripts omit *against you*)" (Matt. 18:15). In this manner, not to involve others unnecessarily. "If he listens to you, you have won your brother over."

"But if he will not listen, take one or two others along, so that every matter may be established by the testimony of two or three witnesses." This, in turn, provides a reality check, which can result in reconciliation.

"If he refuses to listen to them, tell it to the church; and if he refuses to listen even to the church, treat him as you would a pagan or tax collector." Not in an abusive fashion, but as one not of the household of faith.

Finally, guidance may require making choices among plausible options. Now Paul and his companions traveled throughout the region of Phrygia and Galatia, "having been kept by the Holy Spirt from preaching the word in the province of Asia." Since details are lacking, we can only speculate as to how they were prohibited. It was likely some combination of overt circumstances, and intuitive impressions.

When they came to the border of Mysia, they tried to enter Bithynia, "but the Spirit of Jesus would not allow them to. So they passed by Mysia and went down to Troas." Thus God's leading seems to consist of a combination of open and closed doors, although these may not have been evident to those insensitive to the Spirit's leading. Then, too, the lesser good may keep us from the greater good.

During the night, Paul had a vision concerning a Macedonian man begging him: "Come over to Macedonia and help us." After the apostle had reported the vision, he and his companions made ready to leave for Macedonia. This perhaps implies that they conferred together before making this decision. In any case, the vision was something extraordinary, and not likely to be duplicated except on extremely rare occasions.

Thus primed, we turn our attention to the Beatitudes. We are alerted at the outset to the fact that Jesus taught his disciples in the presence of the multitude. In proverbial terms, the line was drawn in the sand—distinguishing Jesus and his disciples from the remainder. Until recently, the disciples were part of the collective multitude, but now they must contend with the cost of discipleship. Likewise, the multitude must have sensed something of the separation, and wondered what to make of it.

Jesus' words have resonated down through the ages. "Blessed are the poor in spirit, for theirs is the kingdom of heaven" (Matt. 5:2). Those who are genuinely blessed are not the privileged, as commonly supposed, but the contrite. For two reasons that come readily to mind. First, the more we have, the more we want, and the less satisfied with what we have (cf. Eccles. 5:10). Second, what matters most is cultivating a vital relationship with the Almighty and others. As Jesus allowed earlier, "Man does not live on bread alone, but on every word that comes from the mouth of God" (Matt. 4:4; cf. Deut. 8:3).

"Blessed are those who mourn, for they will be comforted." In contrast to the affluent, who have already received their consolation (cf. Luke 6:24).

"Blessed are the meek, for they will inherit the earth." Such as are not greedy and grasping. In this connection, Jesus declared: "Whoever finds his life will lose it, and whoever loses his life for my sake will find it" (Matt. 10:39).

"Blessed are those who hunger and thirst for righteousness, for they will be filled." This, in turn, recalls a poignant text from the Psalter: "As the deer pants for streams of water, so my soul pants for you, O God" (42:1). In this regard, Augustine observed that man was created with a need only God could satisfy.

"Blessed are the merciful, for they will be shown mercy." Jesus subsequently elaborated. "For in the same way you judge others, you will be judged and with the measure you use, it will be measured to you" (Matt.. 7:2). Likewise, "Do not be deceived: God cannot be mocked. A man reaps what he sows" (Gal. 7:2).

"Blessed are the pure in heart, for they will see God." Whose devotion is unadulterated, and intent free from ulterior motives. Then, too, where hypocrisy is strikingly absent.

"Blessed are the peacemakers, for they will be called the sons of God." "It is clear that 'peacemakers' designates not those who live in peace, enjoying its fruits, but those who devote themselves to the hard work of reconciling hostile individuals, families, groups, and nations."[6]

"Blessed are those who are persecuted because of righteousness, for theirs is the kingdom of God." "What is going to harm you if you are eager to do good?" Peter inquires. "But even if you suffer for what is right, you are blessed" (1 Peter 3:13).

Jesus thereby concludes his discourse concerning the Beatitudes. "The first four have emphasized the persecution condition of Jesus' disciples. The latter four have emphasized the ethical qualities which led to their persecution. Accordingly, the first four end on the note of righteousness as divine justice, the second four on the note of righteousness as good conduct."[7]

Furthermore, four implied exhortations may be pointed out. First, live in community. Where persons are reciprocally available, and individually and collectively open to God's gracious initiatives.

Second, live expectantly. The best is yet to come; in light of the Lord's return, and pervasive shalom. All things considered, press on—as would one who is running a race (cf. Heb. 12:1).

Third, live humbly. Do not pretend to be something other than what we are. Conversely, neither be self-effacing—since this amounts to a negative expression of pride (involving undue obsession with self).

Finally, live solicitously. Register concern for others, whether of the household of faith or some other. Do good whenever the opportunity affords itself. Render service gladly. As popularly expressed, walk the walk.

22

IN THE BEGINNING

This is the first of two brief illustrative studies, concerning Genesis and Luke/Acts. These belong to the genre designated as *special hermeneutics*. Otherwise, they will speak for themselves.

Genesis is the first of a five-volume set constituting the *Pentateuch*. The latter is traditionally associated with Moses, and designated by the term *Torah* (teaching, law). In this regard, we read that Joshua copied "the law of Moses, which he had written" (Josh. 8:32).

Critical scholars have proposed an elaborate source theory to alternatively account for the text. Herbert Wolf summarizes its current status:

New approaches to the study of the Pentateuch continue to be developed, some as firmly committed to the non-Mosaic character of these books as Wellhausen was a century ago. Yet at the same time the case for the Mosaic authorship has been strengthened by our increasing knowledge about the history, culture, and religion of the ancient Near East.[1]

Qualifications aside, it would seem that the

Pentateuch is a homogeneous composition in five volumes, and not an agglomeration of separate and perhaps only rather casually related works. It described, against an accredited historical background, the manner in which God revealed Himself to man and chose the Israelites for special service and witness to the world and in the course of human history.[2]

The title *Genesis* derives from the initial expression "In the beginning." This appears to correspond to "the time of the gods" in pagan literature. In particular, it pre-dated the advent of humans. In this instance, God existed in solitary splendor.

A general outline of the text is as follows:

PRIMEVAL TIMES:

Account of Creation (1:1-2:3)
Probation and Fall (1:4-3:24)
Aftermath (4:1-11:32)

PATRIARCHAL TIMES:

Abraham Narrative (12-20)
Isaac Narrative (21-26)
Jacob Narrative (27-36)
Joseph Narrative (37-50)

Account of Creation (1:1-2:3). "In the beginning God created the heavens and the earth." While not explicitly stated, it is elsewhere implied that God created *ex nihilo* (out of nothing) (cf. Psa. 148:5; Prov. 8:22-27). *The heavens and the earth* is a comprehensive idiom, anticipating our space-time continuum. As quoted in an earlier context: "These days most cosmologists and astronomers back the theory that there was indeed a creation, about eighteen billion years ago, when the physical universe burst into existence in an awesome explosion popularly known as the 'big bang'."[3] Some insist on a more recent origin.

"Now the earth was formless and empty, darkness was over the surface of the deep, and the spirit of God was hovering over the waters." In terms of idiom, this resembled clay which the potter had cast, in anticipation of creating a vessel. The end result would be a testimony to his artistic expertise.

The formula "and God said" is repeated in each instance by way of emphasis. The expression is taken as a sovereign mandate, calculated to achieve the purpose for which it was intended. This, in turn, solicits divine approval. Then, in conclusion, "God saw all that he had made, and it was very good."

The term *yom* (day) can be employed as consecutive or intermittent twenty-four hour days, or as an indeterminate period of time. If the latter, then presumably as one of the days of creation. The qualifying reference to *evening and morning* is perhaps indicative of the twenty-four hour alternative.

Man (generic, embracing male and female) appears as a climax to God's creative activity. As expressed, "So God created man in his own image, in the image of God he created them, male and female he created them." It has been suggested that man images God by way of being able to commune with him, in being delegated responsibility to supervise creation, and/or in ways that makes this possible. Most likely, all the above.

Probation and Fall (1:4-3:24). The Lord God planted a garden to the east, toward the rising sun. The idiom may convey the notion of inviting opportunity. After that, he situated man within this ideal setting, with the instruction to tend it.

"You are free to eat from any tree of the garden," the Lord God said to him;

"but you must not eat from the tree of the knowledge of good and evil, for when you eat of it you will surely die" (2:16-17). Since the Almighty had provided ample provision, there was no excuse for distrusting his good intent.

The sole prohibition concerned the tree of *the knowledge of good and evil.* While variously understood, this seems to be a comprehensive idiom—not unlike when we say "as far as it is from the east to the west." If so, eating of the tree would be tantamount to opting for autonomy.

"It is not good for the man to be alone," God concluded. "I will make a helper suitable for him" (2:18). So the Lord God caused man to fall into a deep sleep, and formed woman from his rib. We are thus alerted to the fact that they were distinctive from all the other creatures and ideally compatible. In this regard, they are meant to complement one another, rather than compete. "For this reason a man will leave his father and mother and be united to his wife, and they will become one flesh."

Now the serpent was more crafty than any of the other animals. "Did God really say, "You must not eat from any tree in the garden?" he impugned the Almighty's intention. When Eve verified that this was the case, the serpent protested: "You will not die. For God knows that when you eat of it your eyes will be opened, and you will be like God, knowing good and evil" In this manner, they would be able to determine for themselves what was right and wrong.

When she saw that the fruit was not only good to eat and pleasant to behold, but desirable for gaining wisdom, she took some and ate it. She also gave some to her husband, and he ate of it. They thereby lost their pristine innocense. Their "new consciousness of good and evil was both like and unlike the divine knowledge (3:22), differing from it and from innocense as a sick man's achieving awareness of his body differs both from the insight of the physician and unconcern of the man in health."[4] So it was that when they heard the sound of the Lord God walking in the garden in the cool of the evening, they hid from him.

The man was quick to blame the woman, and more indirectly God for introducing the temptress. The woman passed on the blame to the serpent for having deceived her. Whereupon, God sentenced the serpent to grovel in the dirt, and put enmity between its offspring and that of the woman. While the struggle would continue relentlessly, man would eventually strike a mortal blow. Thus are we alerted early on that God would redeem his people.

Woman was told that she would experience increased pain in childbirth, and be dependent on her husband. Man was informed that he would be involved in grievous toil all the days of his life. None of the perpetrators escaped unscathed.

"The man has now become like one of us, knowing good and evil," the Lord God observed. "He must not be allowed to reach out his hand and take also from the tree of life" (3:22). Since this would indefinitely perpetuate this sorry state of affairs. So the Lord God banished them from the garden, and stationed cherubim to keep them from returning.

Aftermath (4:1-11:32). With notable exceptions, things went from bad to worse. Eve gave birth to two sons: Cain the elder and Abel his sibling. While both made offerings to the Lord, Abel's resembled that which one would provide for an honored guest, while Cain's offering was perfunctory. As a result, God was pleased with Abel's devotion, but not that of Cain.

Cain was exceedingly angry, and slew his brother. At this, God inquired of him:

"Where is your brother Abel?" This was by way of demanding accountability.

"I don't know," he replied. "Am I my brother's keeper?" He meant to give the impression that he could not be expected to keep track of his sibling.

The Lord then pronounced a curse on Cain. The ground, which received his sibling's blood, would no longer readily yield crops for him. As a result, he would become *a restless wanderer on the earth*. Even so, God put a sign on him as protection against retaliation.

His descendant Lamech subsequently boasted to his wives: "I have killed a man for wounding me, a young man for injuring me. If Cain is avenged seven times, then Lamech seventy-seven times" (4:23-24). "(His) taunt-song reveals the swift progress of sin. Where Cain had succumbed to it Lamech exalts in it, where Cain had sought protection Lamech looks around for provocation; the savage disproportion of killing a mere lad for a mere wound is the whole point of his boast."[5]

Eve again bore a son, called *Seth*. He and his posterity emulated Abel. This was eminently borne out by Enoch, who was said to have walked with God. Nevertheless, *the sons of God* opted to intermingle with *the sons of men*, likely a merger of the two lines of descent.

"The Lord saw how great man's wickedness on the earth had become, and that every inclination of the thoughts of his heart was only evil all the time" (6:5). One could hardly imagine a more sweeping indictment. In contrast, Noah found favor in the sight of the Lord.

So the Lord instructed Noah to build an ark for the saving of his family, and the perpetuation of animal species. Once they had entered the ark, there was a great deluge. When the waters had receded, God established a covenant with Noah and his posterity.

The Table of the Nations (10-11) provides a helpful transition.

> First, the human race is united by virtue of being one family. Such was already implied by the monotheistic orientation of Scripture. Second, the human race is separated and dispersed as a result of its defiant effort in seeking to erect the tower of Babel. It had consequently failed in the attempt to usurp God's rightful place at life's center. Third, the nations one and all stand within the divine structure of blessings and curses set forth in the covenant with Noah.[6]

We will elaborate on the Tower of Babel incident only in passing. All persons spoke the same language, and congregated in a certain valley. "Come," they urged one another, "let us build ourselves a city, with a tower that reaches to the heavens, so that we may make a name for ourselves and not be scattered over the face of the whole earth" (11:4). It was a pretentious enterprise and an affront to the Almighty. So it was that the Lord confused their language, and they were scattered to the winds. The stage was now set for the entrance of the patriarchs.

Abraham Narrative (12-20). God subsequently enjoined Abraham, "Leave your country, your people and your father's household and go to the land I will show you" (12:1). Each injunction was meant to increasingly accent the radical disjuncture from his former way of life.

There would, as previously observed, be rich dividends. "I will make you into a great nation and I will bless you; I will make your name great, and you will be a blessing," the Lord informed him. As a matter of record, "By faith Abraham, when called to go to a place he would after receive as an inheritance, obeyed and went, even though he did not know where he was going" (Heb. 11:8).

It would be an eventful pilgrimage. The text provides the following examples:

Sojourn in Egypt (12:10-20)
Rescue of Lot (13:1-14:24)
Ratification of the Covenant (15:1-21)
Account of Hagar and Ishmael (16:1-16)
Confirmation of the Covenant (17:1-27)
Destruction of Sodom and Gomorrah (18:1-19:38)
Encounter with Abimelech (20:1-18)
Thereafter, as associated with Isaac.

The ratification of the covenant will serve as a representative instance. Now the word of the Lord came to Abram (Abraham) in a vision: "Do not be afraid Abram. I am your shield, your very great reward" (15:1).

"O Sovereign Lord," the patriarch complained. "You have given me no children, so a servant in my household will be my heir."

"Look up at the heavens and count the stars—if indeed you can count them," the Lord countered. "So shall your offspring be."

Accordingly, "Abraham believed the Lord, and he credited it to him as righteousness." "The editorial comment with which the first scene closes points out that Abram's silence showed his faith in the promises just made to him. Without the remark, an element of ambiguity would have surrounded (his) reaction."[7]

Issac Narrative (22-26). Sarah conceived and bore a son, who they named *Isaac*. It came to pass that God meant to test Abraham's fidelity. "Take your only son, Isaac, whom you love," the Lord enjoined him, and "sacrifice him as a burnt offering" (22:1). While Abraham would have been familiar with the practice of child sacrifice, he was still learning the ways of the Almighty.

Early the next day, they set out for the place the Lord had designated. On the third day, the patriarch would make it out in the distance. At this, he instructed his servants to await their return. Hebrews observes, "Abraham reasoned that God could raise the dead, and figuratively speaking, he did receive Isaac back from the dead" (11:19).

When they reached the location, Abraham prepared an altar and placed his son on it. He was about to slay the lad, when he heard a voice from heaven: "Do not lay a hand on the boy. Now I know that you fear God, because you have not withheld from me your son, your only son."

The patriarch looked up, and saw a ram caught by its horns in a thicket. He sacrificed it instead of his offspring. This, in turn, took the form of a proverbial saying: "On the mountain of the Lord it will be provided."

When Abraham was well along in life, he charged his chief servant with obtaining a wife for Isaac from his extended family. It was common practice, as a means of assuring the couple's compatibility and support structure.

"O Lord, God of my master Abraham," the servant petitioned, "give me success today, and show kindness to my master Abraham" (24:12). When Rebekah came to draw water, he knew by pre-arrangement that she was the one. "So she became (Isaac's) wife, and he loved her; and (he) was comforted after his mother's death." In this manner, the promise was passed on from one generation to the next.

Jacob Narrative (27-36). When Isaac was elderly and his eye-sight impaired, he summoned his elder son Esau. "Now then," he implored, "go out to the open country to hunt game and bring it back" (27:3). Rebekah overheard what he had said, and conspired with Jacob to deceive her husband. He pretended to be his sibling, and thereby receive the blessing intended for the elder son. Esau was furious, and determined to kill him once their father had passed away, and the days of mourning were finished.

Alarmed with the prospect, his mother urged him to flee to her brother Laban for security. Along the way, he stopped for the night. There he had a dream concerning a stairway resting on earth, with its top reaching to heaven, and the angels of God ascending and descending on it. Above it stood the Lord (28:12-13).

"The ladder or stairway that Jacob sees in his dream is the passageway between heaven and earth. (These were) built to provide a way for the deity to descend to the temple and town"[8] Jacob would have been familiar with this imagery derived from ancient Mesopotamia. Upon awakening, he reflected: "Surely the Lord is in this place, and I was not aware of it."

Jacob remained with Laban for an extended period of time, after which he spirited his wives Leah and Rachel away—with the intent to return to his parental home. Pursued by Laban, they agreed to go their separate ways. Subsequently, Jacob was reconciled to his estranged brother.

Joseph Narrative (37-50). Now Israel (Jacob) loved Joseph more than his other sons, since he was birthed late in life. His brothers were secretly jealous of him. Given the opportunity, they sold him into slavery and reported that he was killed by a ferocious animal.

Meanwhile, Joseph was taken down into Egypt, where he was sold to Potiphar—an Egyptian official. The Lord was with him, so that he prospered (cf. 39:2). However, Potiphar's wife tried to seduce him. Failing in her attempt, she reported that Joseph had attempted to rape her. He was cast into prison.

During his imprisonment, Joseph interpreted dreams for two inmates. One of them, who had been the chief cupbearer for Pharaoh, was restored to his position. When the king had perplexing dreams, Joseph was promptly summoned.

It turned out that the dreams concerned an impending famine. Pharaoh was duly impressed by the interpretation, and put Joseph in charge of his affairs. As a result, Joseph had supplies stored to see the people through the difficult days that lay ahead.

When his brothers came to Egypt to replenish their food supply, Joseph revealed his identity to them. He assured them that he meant them no harm: for while they had intended evil by selling him into slavery, God meant to bring about good. It came to pass that the Israelites found sanctuary in Egypt.

Joseph lived a full life. "I am about to die," he observed. "But God will surely come to your aid and take you up out of this land to the land he promised on oath to Abraham, Isaac, and Jacob" (50:24-25). Accordingly, he enjoined them to take his remains with them. All things considered, while the patriarchs were not always faithful, they were men of faith. It was for this reason that the author of Hebrews extols them.

23

LUKE/ACTS

Luke/Acts is a two-volume set. Initially, Luke sets about to record the life and ministry of Jesus. After that, he expands with an account of the early Christian fellowship—with emphasis on the work of the apostles.

Luke is introduced as a companion of the apostle Paul. He was likely a God-fearing Gentile, and as such familiar with the prophetic writings, but not disposed to becoming a Jewish convert. He is referred to as "our dear friend Luke, the doctor" (Col. 4:4), which may account for his attention to detail.

I elswhere made mention of some of the principles that might profitably be kept in mind when interpreting this two-fold text. As paraphrased,

1. Luke/Acts exhibits a dual concern with the life of Christ and the early church. These must be viewed in constructive tension.
2. This led us to ponder why of all that Jesus said and did, these entries were preserved. In general terms, we may conclude that it served to provide a more precise understanding, and serve the needs of the emerging fellowship.
3. The roots of the text are planted in the Old Testament Scripture, the stock shoots up through inter-testament times, and it flourishes during the turbulent generation stretching from Caesar Augustus to Nero. We see a corresponding shift in cultural setting, from Palestine and Judaism to Rome and paganism.
4. The gospel provides an inextricable bond between the two volumes. In the process, they document how a seemingly insignificant Jewish sect was rapidly becoming a cosmopolitan movement of amazing proportion.
5. Other observations noted in passing include Luke's concern for detail, his apologetic for the faith, and his emphasis on the critical role of prayer.[1]

An abbreviated outline will suffice:

Gospel of Luke

Preface (1:1-4)
Advent of Jesus as the Messiah (1:5-4:15)
His Public Ministry (4:16-18:30)
Passion Account (18:31-24:53)

Acts of the Apostles

Introduction (1:1-11)
Jerusalem (1:12-8:3)
Judea and Samaria (8:4-11:18)
To the Ends of the Earth (11:19-21:16)
Imprisonment (21:17-28:31)

Preface to Volume One (1:1-4). Luke notes at the outset that others have attempted to give an account of the life and ministry of Jesus. "Therefore," he continues, "since I myself have carefully investigated everything from the beginning, it seemed good also for me to write an orderly account for you, most excellent Theophilus, so that you may know the certainty of the things you have been taught" (1:3-4). *Theophilus* was perhaps a patron, or simply a personification.

Luke does not explicate what he means by *an orderly account*. With little exception, the text could be arranged chronologically.

Advent of Jesus the Messiah (1:5-4:15). The births of both John the Baptist and Jesus are foretold. In a manner of speaking, there were rumors of angels abroad, conveying the good news that a savior was to be birthed.

Joseph and Mary subsequently made their way to Bethlehem to be registered, since Joseph was of the lineage of David. "Salma, son of Caleb, was designated *the father of Bethlehem* (1 Chron. 2:51). It was also home for a young Levite who served as Micah's priest (Judg. 17:8), along with Boaz, Ruth, Obed, and Jesse—the father of David (Ruth 4:11; 1 Sam. 16:1, 4)."[2]

Bethlehem was at the time an unpretentious village. Its main claim to fame was its association with David and hence the anticipation that the Messiah would be born there. As for the latter, "But you, Bethlehem Ephrathah, though you are small among the clans of Judah, out of you will come for me one who will be ruler over Israel, whose origins are from old, from ancient times" (Micah 5:2).

There were shepherds living out in the field nearby, keeping watch over their flocks at night. An angel appeared to them, the glory of the Lord shone around them, and they were terrified. "Do not be afraid," the angel assured them. "I bring you good news of great joy that will be for all the people. Today in the town of David a Savior has been born to you; he is Christ the Lord" (2:10-11).

Suddenly a great heavenly host appeared with the angel, praising God and saying: "Glory to God in the highest, and on earth peace to men on whom his favor rests." When the shepherds had seen for themselves, they returned praising God—which Luke implies should be par for the course.

Jesus' legal parents are depicted as devout Jews. They had their son circumcised, and presented him at the temple. Their offering on the latter occasion indicates that they were of modest means.

While in the temple precinct, Simeon (among those who waited for *the consolation of Israel*) took the child in his arms, saying: "Sovereign Lord, as you have promised, you now dismiss your servant in peace. For my eyes have seen your salvation, which you have prepared in the sight of all people, a light for revelation to the Gentiles, and the glory to your people Israel" (2:29-32).

Every year Jesus' parents went up to Jerusalem for the Feast of Passover. When he was twelve years of age, they left for their return journey—supposing that he was with relatives or friends. When by nightfall he was not to be found, they rushed back to Jerusalem. After three days, they found him in the temple precinct; listening to the rabbis and asking them questions. Persons were amazed at his insight. "Why were you looking for me?" Jesus inquired. "Didn't you know that I had to be in my Father's house?" Luke editorializes, "But they did not understand what he was saying to them."

After that, he went down to Nazareth and was obedient to them—as admonished in the Decalogue (cf. Exod. 20:12). Accordingly, "Jesus grew in wisdom and stature, and in favor with God and man." In other words, he matured in all respects.

Some time later, John the Baptist came preaching "a baptism of repentance for the forgiveness of sins" (3:3). Jesus also came to be baptized. When John was reluctant to do so, he insisted—apparently so as to identify with those he came to redeem. Whereupon, the Holy Spirit descended in a form similar to that of a dove, and a voice from heaven declared: "You are my son, whom I love; with you I am well pleased." We are to understand this as an anointing for his ministry.

After this, Jesus was led into the wilderness, where he was tempted by the adversary for forty days and nights. In context, this appears as a calculated effort to divert him from his mission. In any case, Jesus remained resolute, citing appropriate scriptures in the process. He was about thirty years of age when he began his ministry. This was in keeping with the traditional time for entering into public service (cf. Gen. 41:46; Num. 4:3, 23; 2 Sam. 5:4).

His public ministry (4:16-18:30). Jesus returned to Galilee in the power of the Spirit, taught in the synagogues, and was well received. He returned to Nazareth, and made his way to the synagogue—as was his custom. When they handed him the Isaiah scroll, he located the place where it was written: "The Spirit of the Lord is on me, because he has anointed me to preach good news to the poor. He has sent me to proclaim freedom for the prisoners and recovery of sight for the blind, to release the oppressed, to proclaim the acceptable year of the Lord's favor (4:18-19; cf. Isa. 61:1-2).

It consisted of Jubilee imagery crafted for Messianic times. When Jesus had finished reading, he returned the scroll and sat down—in anticipation of giving instruction. He began by saying, "Today this scripture is fulfilled in your hearing."

As allowed earlier, their cordial welcome was based on a parochial understanding of his mission. Then, when he rebuked them for their lack of responsiveness, they were furious with him. They meant to kill him, but "he walked through the crowd and went on his way." Luke offers no explanation.

The fact that Jesus taught with authority first caught the attention of the populace. In this regard, he diverted from the common practice of citing religious precedent. They were at a loss to know what to make of it.

He soon began to perform miracles. Some of these concerned nature, such as the stilling of a storm. Others resulted in physical healing. Still others involved exorcism. These served to authenticate his ministry.

Then, too, they not uncommonly served as salvation parables. So it was when Jesus restored the eyesight of a blind person, it lent itself to a spiritual application.

It comes as no surprise that Jesus did and said many other things that are not recorded in Luke's account. Initially, one would suppose that some events are included simply because they were especially significant. Such as the above account of Jesus' return to his synagogue in Nazareth, in that it puts his public ministry in context.

Other instances may have been little more than representative. One incident might serve as well as another, but this or that was recalled by Luke—so as to characterize Jesus' public ministry. In this manner, the writer meant to provide an accurate account—not unduly biased by certain more prominent features.

Luke's choice of material also reveals a current agenda. This is especially striking in the way he illustrates the universal significance of the gospel. Thus Jesus is criticized for his cordial relationship with *sinners* (non-observant Jews), in a manner that anticipates a subsequent outreach to Gentiles. Certain of his parables were along this line as well, such as those concerning the lost son, sheep, and coin.

Incidently, a few instances appear to be primarily for literary purposes. For instance, when a segment of Jesus' teaching is set forth between two travel accounts. Or when a different location is abruptly introduced.

Of course, one must not rule out the guidance of the Spirit in all this. He reportedly works in mysterious ways, to accomplish his redemptive purposes. Accordingly, Luke was not strictly speaking left on his own to make critical decisions.

Then, finally, one would suppose that some combination of the above factors were involved. This would be in a creative manner, in keeping the human potential as prompted by the divine. Were we to know all that is involved, it would no doubt appear still more amazing.

In any case, opposition to Jesus' ministry was building. In proverbial terms, the handwriting was on the wall. Even so, Jesus zealously took the lead—his disciples strung out behind him.

Passion Account (18:31-24:53). The term *passion* is used to denote those portions of the gospels which lead up to Jesus' demise. This is characterized by his resolve to do his Father's will at all cost

Jesus took his disciples aside to inform them: "We are going to Jerusalem, and everything that is written by the prophets concerning the Son of Man will be fulfilled. He will be handed over to the Gentiles. They will mock him, insult him, spit on him, flog him, and kill him. On the third day he will rise again" (18:31-32).

It was about noon and there was darkness over the land. It would remain so until Jesus expired, some three hours later. Then, too, the curtain of the temple was rent in two, suggesting access to the Almighty. While the *darkness* is variously interpreted, it would seem indicative of the present, evil world. All things considered, it appears to suggest that the spiritual stubble had entered its critical stage.

"Father," Jesus cried out, "into your hands I commit my spirit" (23:48; cf. Psa. 31:5). It was expressive of a confident trust. He had successfully completed his mission.

The attending centurion, observing what had transpired, declared: "Surely this was a righteous man." Those looking on beat their breasts as a sign of remorse, and took their departure. Those *who knew him* stood at a discreet distance, as witnesses to the event.

Joseph, a member of the Sanhedrin, requested Jesus' body in order to give it a proper burial. It was laid in a rock tomb. Women prepared spices and perfumes in keeping with burial practices, but tarried until the Sabbath was over. Then, on the first day of the week, they returned to the tomb—only to find it empty. While they were still wondering what had happened, two translucent figures appeared. "Why do you look for the living among the dead?" they inquired. "He is not here; he has risen!" (24:5-6).

The same day two of Jesus' disciples were making their way to Emmaus, about seven miles from Jerusalem. As they were discussing what had taken place, Jesus joined them. However, they did not recognize him. As for apt commentary, "Notice that in the Gospels the risen Christ appears to the disciples, not to unbelievers on the street and in synagogues to frighten them into an acquiescing faith. After instruction in Scripture and the Lord's Supper (or common meal), the two disciples recognize Jesus."[3]

Jesus subsequently appeared to others. Then, when he had led them out into the vicinity of Bethany, he lifted up his hands and blessed them. As he did so, he was taken up into the heavens. Whereupon, they worshiped him and returned to Jerusalem with exceeding joy. There they remained in the temple, praising God. Thus Luke concludes his initial volume.

* * *

Introduction to Volume 2 (1:1-11). "In my former book, Theophilus, I wrote about all that Jesus began to do and teach until the day he was take up to heaven," Luke recalls (Acts 1:1-2). In this connection, "Christianity is a historical religion.

It is a religion not based primarily on an idea or philosophy. If you take away the history—as some have tried to do—to a religion of mere ethics or ideas—Christianity evaporates."[4]

"It is not for you to know the times or dates the Father has set by his own authority," Jesus confided in his disciples. "But you will receive power when the Holy Spirit comes upon you, and you will be my witnesses in Jerusalem, Judea and Samaria, and to the ends of the earth."

> In particular, their calling would necessitate obedience, service, and suffering. Obedience first, since it was in response to Jesus' injunction; service second, because it requires putting the welfare of others above that of themselves; suffering last, in that Christ calls his disciples to take up their cross and follow him.[5]

Jerusalem (1:12-8:3). "When the day of Pentecost came, they were all together in one place" (2:1). It was so-called since the festival occurred the fiftieth day after Passover. Originally a harvest celebration, it would come to be associated with the giving of the Torah.

"Suddenly a sound like the blowing of a violent wind came from heaven and filled the whole house where they were sitting. They saw what seemed to be tongues of fire that separated and came to rest on each of them." At this, they were filled with the Holy Spirit, and some (more likely) or all began to speak with other tongues. This could be a reference to ecstatic utterance, a foreign language, or some combination of the two. In any case, it would appear evident that Luke means this as a symbolic reversal of the diffusion of language at the Tower of Babel.

As a result, "They devoted themselves to the apostles' teaching and to the fellowship, to the breaking of bread and to prayer" (2:42). Everyone was filled with awe, and many miracles were done by the apostles, They bonded together, and shared generously. Then, too, the Lord added to their number daily.

Conversely, problems arose. From without, involving persecution by the authorities. From within, in the equitable distribution of charitable funds. In either instance, it presented a challenge to the fledgling community. Meanwhile, they were slow to undertake the task of heralding the gospel beyond the confines of Jerusalem, until persecution dispersed them into the surrounding regions.

Judea and Samaria (8:4-11:8). "Those who had been scattered preached the word wherever they went" (8:4). Philip went down to a city in Samaria, and proclaimed Christ there. When the people heard what he had to say, and saw the miraculous signs he performed, they greatly rejoiced.

He subsequently encountered an Ethiopian official, who was presumably a God-fearing Gentile. The latter was reading concerning the Suffering Servant, and inquired as to whom it referred. This resulted in his being baptized, on confession of faith in Jesus as the Messiah.

Meanwhile, Saul had received authorization to carry his persecution of the church to Damascus. As he neared his destination, a bright light from heaven shone around him, and a voice inquired: "Saul, Saul, why do you persecute me?" (9:4).

"Who are you, Lord?" Saul inquired.

"I am Jesus, whom you are persecuting," the voice replied. "Now get up and go into the city, and you will be told what you must do." In remarkably short order, the former persecutor of the church became its chief advocate.

There was also a devout God-fearing centurion named *Cornelius*. God prompted Peter to share the gospel with those assembled in his home. When this came to the attention of some of the Jewish believers, they protested: "You went into the house of uncircumcised men and ate with them." But when the apostle explained to them what had transpired, "they had no further objections and praised God, saying, 'So then, God has granted even the Gentiles repentance unto life.'"

To the Ends of the Earth (11:19-21:16). There were in the church of Syrian Antioch a cosmopolitan group of prophets and teachers, suggesting an ingathering of Gentiles. The Holy Spirit instructed them, "Set apart Barnabas and Saul for the work to which I have called them" (13:2). So after they had fasted and prayed, they commissioned them for the service to which they were called.

They set sail for Cyprus, where they were summoned by the proconsul to hear *the word of God*. Elymus the sorcerer attempted to turn him away from the faith, and was temporarily blinded as a rebuke.

Upon their return to the mainland, they made their way to Pisidian Antioch. Invited to address those gathered in the synagogue, Paul gave what might be construed as a typical message for those who were schooled in the prophets. It consisted of a review of God's previous activity, leading up to the proclamation of the gospel.

Nearly the whole city turned out to hear them the next Sabbath, inciting the Jews to jealously. "We had to speak the word of God to you first," the missionaries allowed. "Since you reject it and do not consider yourselves worthy of eternal life, we now turn to the Gentiles" (13:46). When the Gentiles heard this, they rejoiced, and the word spread throughout the region. They continued on to Iconium, and then Lystra.

Sometime later, Paul and his companions responded to an appeal to minister in Macedonia. He and Silas were incarcerated in Philippi, but delivered in miraculous fashion. In the process, the jailor and his family embraced the faith.

After eventful visits to Thessalonica and Berea, Paul arrived in advance of his companions at Athens. "It was hundreds of years after Athens' golden age that Paul visited the city and preached the sermon recorded in Acts 17, but (it) was still a strikingly beautiful city as well as the intellectual capital of the ancient world."[6]

The apostle was subsequently interrogated by the Areopagus, the esteemed traditional court of the city. On this occasion, he delivered what would perhaps qualify as a characteristic approach to raw Gentiles. This was by way of allusion to the High God, who created life and providentially sustains it—in anticipation of the anticipated advent of the Messiah.

Paul continued on to Corinth, where he worked for a while in his trade—until the arrival of Silas and Timothy. After that, he gave himself without reserve to the ministry. He stayed on for some time, before working his way back to Antioch.

The final phase of his missionary activity focused largely on Ephesus. Here he invoked the ire of the artisans, who made their living from making religious artifacts. These, in turn, stirred up the populace. Consequently, Paul soon took his leave.

Imprisonment (21:17-28:31). Drawing upon similarities between the experience of Jesus and Paul, this segment is sometimes identified as *the passion of Paul*. Like Jesus, the apostle was forewarned of his coming arrest (cf. 21:11). Like Jesus, he continued on to Jerusalem. Like Jesus, they imprisoned him. Like Jesus, this would eventually lead to his demise—although at a later time.

This allowed the apostle to give a spirited defense: before the Jerusalem populace (22:1-21), the Sanedrin (22:30-23:10), Felix (24:1-26), Festuca (25:1-12), and Agrippa (26:1-32). "Do you think that in such a short time you can persuade me to be a Christian?" Agrippa contemptuously inquired.

"Short time or long," Paul replied; "I pray God that not only you but all who are listening to me today may become what I am, except for these chains."

The apostle appealed his case to Caesar. In transit, his ship was lost. Upon arrival, he was placed under house arrest. This allowed him to continue preaching the gospel. While the narrative terminates at this point, it appears that Paul was subsequently released, only to again be imprisoned and executed. In fitting conclusion, "these two things—the preacher's boldness and the proclamation to all—are among the lasting impressions of the book. They stand, perhaps as a reproach, certainly as a challenge and a charter to all who now read it."[7]

ENDNOTES

PART ONE

Preface

1. Gordon Fee, *The First Epistle to the Corinthians*, p. 105.
2. Peter Berger, *The Sacred Canopy*, p. 24.
3. George A. F. Knight, *Isaiah 56-66: The New Israel*, p. 103.

Chapter 1: Ultimate Mystery

1. J. A. Motyer, "Mystery," *Evangelical Dictionary of Theology* (Elwell, ed.), p. 741.
2. Walton, John and Victor Matthews (eds.), *Genesis-Deuteronomy*, p. 87.
3. R. Alan Cole, *Exodus*, p. 65.
4. Ibid., p. 75.
5. Charles Pfeiffer, *Old Testament History*, pp. 357-358.
6. Abraham Heschel, *The Prophets*, p. 4.
7. Ibid., p. 10.
8. David Myers, "The Mystery of the Ordinary," *Psychology of Religion* (Malone, ed.), p. 412.
9. Ibid., p. 410.

Chapter 2: Paradoxical Mystery

1. C. S. Lewis, *Mere Christianity*, p. 138.
2. Robert Mounce, *Matthew*, p. 43.
3. Thomas Kuhn, *The Structure of Scientific Revolutions*, p. 2.
4. Morris Inch, *Exhortations of Jesus According to Matthew* and *Up From the Depths*, p. 9.
5. Mounce, *op. cit.*, p. 228.
6. Morris Inch, *Signature of the Spirit*, p. 27.
7. I. Howard Marshall, *Acts*, p. 69.

8. Millard Erickson, *God in Three Persons*, p. 12.

9. Ibid., pp. 12-13.

Chapter 3: The Incarnation

1. Donald Hagner, *Hebrews*, p. 79.

2. F. F. Bruce, *Philippians*, p. 71.

3. Leon Morris, *Luke*, p. 81.

4. Joel Green, *The Gospel of Luke*, pp. 215-216.

5. *The Gospel of Infancy*, 13.

6. Green, *op. cit.*, p. 217.

7. Morris, *op. cit.*, p. 119.

8. C. S. Lewis, *The Screwtape Letters*, p. 20.

9. Ethelbert Stauffer, *Jesus and His Story*, p. 174.

10. Lee Strobel, *The Case For Christ*, p. 195.

11. Ibid., p. 198.

Chapter 4: Illusive Mystery

1. Morris Inch, *Saga of the Spirit*, p. 13.

2. Morris Inch, *Chaos Paradigm: A Theological Exploration*, p. 3.

3. Inch, *Saga of the Spirit*, p. 69.

4. Inch, *Signature of the Spirit*, p. 2.

5. Green, *op. cit.*, p. 185.

6. Craig Evans, *Luke*, p. 82.

7. Green, *op. cit.*, p. 421.

8. Morris Inch, "Manifestation of the Holy Spirit," *The Living and Active Word of God* (Inch and Youngblood, eds.), p. 149.

9. Inch, *Signature of the Spirit*, p. 35.

Chapter 5: Rumor of Angels

1. Francis Anderson, *Job*, p. 84.

2. Ibid.

3. Victor Hamilton, *The Book of Genesis: Chapters 1-17*, p. 210.

4. Joyce Baldwin, *Daniel*, p. 181.

5. 1 Enoch, 40:3, 6.

6. Green, *op. cit.*, p. 780.

7. F. F. Bruce, *The Book of the Acts*, p. 237.

8. Josephus, *The Antiquities of the Jews*, 19, 8, 2.

Chapter 6: Human Mystery

1. James Mays, *Psalms*, p. 69.

2. Ibid.
3. Ibid., p. 70.
4. John Goldingay, *Isaiah*, p. 37.
5. Morris Inch, *In Christ & On Track*, p. 41.
6. Ibid.
7. Mary Evans, *1 and 2 Samuel*, p. 83.
8. Morris Inch, *Devotions With David: A Christian Legacy*, p. 58.

Chapter 7: Universal Mystery

1. Paul Davies, *God & the New Physics*, p. 10.
2. Ibid., p. 11.
3. Mary and John Griffin, *Time and Space*, p. 7.
4. Davies, *op. cit.*, p. 68.
5. Morris Inch, *The High God*, p. 10.
6. Wilhelm Schmidt, *The Origin and Growth of Religion*, p. 270.
7. Davies, *op. cit.*, p. 18.
8. Morris Inch, *Chaos Paradigm: A Theological Exploration*, p. 3.
9. *Theophilus to Autolycus*, XVI, xv.

Chapter 8: Prophecy

1. Derek Kidner, *Proverbs*, p. 59.
2. David Allan Hubbard, *Joel and Amos*, p. 102.
3. Robert Kenneth Harrison, *Introduction to the Old Testament*, p. 887.
4. Abraham Herschel, *The Prophets*, p.10
5. Robert Mounce, *The Book of Revelation*, p. 3.
6 Ibid.
7. Ibid., pp. 3-4.

Chapter 9: The Afterlife

1. C. S. Lewis, *Letters to an American Lady*, June 7, 1959.
2. Oscar Cullmann, "Immortality of the Soul or Resurrection of the Body," *Immortality and Resurrection* (Stendahl, ed.), p. 14.
3. Ibid., p. 15.
4. Millard Erickson, *Christian Theology*, vol. 3, p. 1168.
5. Lim Guef Eng, "Christianity Versus Ancestor Worship in Taiwan," p. 2.
6. Leon Morris, *1 Corinthians*, p. 209.
7. Erickson, *Christian Theology*, vol. 3, p. 1229.
8. Morris Inch, *Whispers of Heaven & Heaven According to Matthew*, p. 31.

Chapter 10: The Miraculous

1. C. S. Lewis, *Miracles,* p. 167.
2. Cole, *op. cit.*, p. 81.
3 Russell Dilday, *1, 2 Kings*, p. 214.
4. Morris Inch, *Man: The Perennial Question*, p. 7.
5. Inch, "Manifestation of the Spirit," p. 49.
6. Helmut Thielicke, *I Believe*, p. 231.
7. Bruce, *The Acts of the Apostles*, p. 313.

Chapter 11: Moral Mystery

1. Augustine, *The Homilies on the First Epistle of John*, 5. 8.
2. J. Harris, C. Brown, and M. Moore, *Joshua, Judges, Ruth*, p. 123.
3. Ibid., p. 139.
4. Arthur Cundall & Leon Morris, *Judges & Ruth*, p. 185.
5. Ibid., p. 194.
6. Inch, *Exhortations of Jesus According to Matthew*, pp. 11-12.
7. Bernard Haring, *The Law of Christ*, vol. 1, p. 99.
8. Leon Morris, *The Gospel According to John*, p. 326.
9. Alvin Schmidt, *Under the Influence*, p. 278.

Chapter 12: Enigmas: Part One

1. Gleason Archer, *Encyclopedia of Bible Difficulties*, p. 46.
2. Herbert Wolf, *An Introduction to the Old Testament Pentateuch*, p. 48.
3. Ibid., p. 104.
4, Archer, *op. cit.*, p. 88.
5. Ibid., p. 113.
6. Walton and Matthews (eds.), *op. cit.*, p. 92.
7. Mary Douglas, *Clean and Unclean*, p. 54.
8. Gary Demarest, *Leviticus*, p. 106.

Chapter 13: Enigmas: Part Two

1. Archer, *op. cit.*, p. 313.
2. Craig Keener, *New Testament*, p. 197.
3. Ethelbert Stauffer, *op. cit.*, p. 33.
4. Joyce Baldwin, *op. cit.*, p. 148.
5. Mounce, *op. cit.*, p. 165.
6. Ibid., p. 253.

Chapter 14: Creative Mystery

1. Robert Seltzer, *Jewish People, Jewish Thought*, p. 197.
2. Walton and Matthews, *op. cit.*, p. 33.
3. Morris Inch, *Service Is As Service Does*, p. 142.
4. Harvey Cox, *Feast of Fools*, p. 62.
5. Inch, *Service Is As Service Does*, p. 143.
6. Bruce, *The Book of the Acts*, p. 201.
7. Ibid., p. 146.
8. George Bernard Shaw, *Saint Joan*, Epilogue.

PART TWO

Chapter 15: All Scripture

1. Justin Martyr, *Dialogue With Trypho*, lxv.
2. Craig Evans, *Luke*, p. 357.
3. Harry Boer, *A Short History of the Early Church*, p. 72.
4. Clement of Alexandria, *Fragments From the Hypotyposes*.
5. Origin, *Commentary on John*, V, 4.
6. George Robinson, *Essential Judaism*, p. 196.

Chapter 16: Salvation History

1. R. Alan Cole, *Exodus*, p. 69.
2. E. John Hamlin, *Judges: At Risk in the Promised Land*, p. 2.
3. Morris Inch, *Scripture As Story*, p. 51.
4. Ibid., p. 115.
5. John Bright, *A History of Israel*, p. 414.
6. Tertullian, *The Apology*, L.

Chapter 17: Fusion of Horizons

1. Friedrich Schleiermacher, *Hermeneutics: The Handwritten Manuscripts*, p. 69.
2. Ibid., p. 47.
3. Anthony Thiselton, *The Two Horizons*, p. 18.
4. Hans-Georg Gadamer, *Method and Truth*, p. 273.
5. Krister Stendahl, *The Bible and the Role of Women*, p. 12.
6. Ibid.
7. Yechiel Eckstein, *How Firm a Foundation*, p. 87.
8. Alvin Schmidt, *Under the Influence*, p. 285.

Chapter 18: Literary Genre

1. Morris Inch, *Understanding Bible Prophesy*, p. 70.
2. Kathleen Farmer, *Proverbs & Ecclesiastes: Who Knows What is Good?*, p. 67.
3. Ben Witherington III, *The Third Search For the Jew of Nazareth*, p. 185.
4. Joel Green, *The Gospel of Luke*, p. 249.
5. Abraham Heschel, *The Prophets*, p. 4.
6. Ibid., p. 10.
7. Joyce Baldwin, *Haggai, Zechariah, Malachi*, p. 252.
8. Josephus, *The Antiquities of the Jews*, 18, 5, 2.
9. R. T. France, *Matthew*, pp. 113-114.
10. Ethelbert Stauffer, *Jesus and His Story*, p. 194.
11. Donald Guthrie, *New Testament Theology*, p. 63.
12. Joyce Baldwin, *Daniel*, p. 87.
13. Donald Hagner, *Matthew 14-28*, p. 688.
14. Josephus, *op.cit.*, 12, 5, 4.
15. Hagner, *op. cit.*, p. 716
16. Robert Mounce, *The Book of Revelation*, p. 3.

Chapter 19: In Context

1. A Berkeley Mickelson, *Interpreting the Bible*, p. 131.
2. Irenaeus, *Against Heresies*, 1, 27, 1.
3. Mickelsen, *op. cit.*, p. 59.
4. John Polkinghorne, *Quarks, Chaos & Christianity*, p. 91
5. *The Martyrdom of Polycarpa*, XI
6. I. Howard Marshall, *The Epistles of John*, p. 226

Chapter 20: Fine Print

1. Mickelsen, *op. cit.*, p. 212.
2. Green, *op. cit.*, p. 414.
3. Baldwin, *Haggai, Zechariah, Malachi*, p. 119.
4. Bruce Vawter and Leslie Hoppe, *Ezekiel: A New Heart*, p. 241.
5. T. Norton Starrett, *How to Understand Your Bible*, p. 123.
6. Cole, *op. cit.*, p. 65.
7. Paul Duke, *Irony in the Fourth Gospel*, p. 45
8. Robert Mounce, *Matthew*, p. 217
9. Inch, *Scripture As Story*, p. 23.

Chapter 21: Walk The Walk

1. Green, *op. cit.*, p. 273.
2. Peter Davids, *James*, p. 65.
3. Morris Inch, *Chaos Paradigm: A Theological Exploration*, p.3.
4. Tertullian, *On Prayer*, xxix.

5. P. M. Forni, *Choosing Civility*, p. 36
6. Douglas Hare, *Matthew*, p. 42.
7. Robert Gundry, *Matthew*, p. 73.

Chapter 22: In The Beginning

1. Herbert Wolf, *An Introduction to the Pentateuch*, p. 78.
2. Roland Kenneth Harrison, *An Introduction to the Old Testament*, p. 541.
3. Paul Davies, *God & the New Physics*, p. 10.
4. Derek Kidner, *Genesis*, p. 69.
5. Ibid., p. 78.
6. Inch, *Scripture As Story*, p. 23 (cf. footnote # 55).
7. Gordon Wenham, *Genesis 1-15*, p. 329
8. John Walton & Victor Matthews, *Genesus-Deuteronomy*, p.39

Chapter 23: Luke/Acts

1. Morris Inch, "Interpreting Luke-Acts," *The Literature and Meaning of Scripture* (Inch and Bulloch, eds.), pp. 183-184.
2. Morris Inch, *Two Gospel Motifs*, p. 6.
3. Fred Braddock, *Luke*, p. 285.
4. James Montgomery Boice, *Acts*, p. 15.
5. Morris Inch, *Signature of the Spirit*, p. 27.
6. Boise, *op. cit.*, p. 294.
7. David Williams, *Acts*, p. 454.

PART ONE

BIBLIOGRAPHY

Anderson, Francis. *Job*. Downers Grove: Inter-Varsity, 1974.

Archer, Gleason. *Encyclopedia of Biblical Difficulties*. Grand Rapids: Zondervan, 1982.

Augustine. *The Homilies of the First Epistle of John*.

Baldwin, Joyce. *Daniel*. Downers Grove: Inter-Varsity, 1978.

Berger, Peter. *The Sacred Canopy*. Garden City: Doubleday, 1967.

Bruce, F. F. *The Book of the Acts*. Grand Rapids: Eerdmans, 1988.

———. *Philippians*. Peabody: Hendrickson, 1993.

Cole, R. Alan. *Exodus*. Downers Grove: Inter-Varsity, 1973.

Cox, Harvey. *The Feast of Fools*. New York: Harper & Row, 1969.

Cullmann, Oscar. "Immortality of the Soul or Resurrection of the Body," *Immortality and Resurrection* (Stendahl, ed.), 9-53.

Cundall, Arthur and Leon Morris. *Judges & Ruth*. Downers Grove: Inter-Varsity, 1968.

Davies, Paul. *God & The New Physics*. New York: Simon & Schuster, 1983.

Demarest, Gary. *Leviticus*. Dallas: Word, 1990.

Dilday, Russell. *1, 2 Kings*. Dallas: Word, 1987.

Douglas, Mary. *Purity and Danger*. New York: Routledge, 1991.

Elwell, Walter (ed.). *Evangelical Dictionary of Theology*. Grand Rapids: Baker, 1984.

Eng, Lim Guef. "Christianity Versus Ancestor Worship in Taiwan" (unpublished).

1 Enoch.

Erickson, Millard. *Christian Theology*, 3 vols. Grand Rapids: Baker, 1985.

———. *God in Three Persons*. Grand Rapids: Baker, 1995.

Evans, Craig. *Luke*. Peabody: Hendrickson, 1990.

Evans, Mary. *1 and 2 Samuel*. Peabody: Hendrickson, 2000.

Fee, Gordon. *The First Epistle to the Corinthians*. Grand Rapids: Eerdmans, 1995.

The Gospel of Infancy.

Goldingay, John. *Isaiah*. Peabody: Hendrickson, 2001.

Green, Joel. *The Gospel of Luke*. Grand Rapids: Eerdmans, 1997.

Gribbin, Mary and John. *Time & Space*. London: DK Publishing, 1994.

Hagner, Donald. *Hebrews*. Peabody: Hendrickson, 1993.

Hamilton, Victor. *The Book of Genesis: Chapters 1-17*. Grand Rapids: Eerdmans, 1990.

Haring, Bernard. *The Law of Christ*, 3 vols. Westminster: Newman, 1961.

Harris, J., C. Brown, and M. Moore. *Joshua, Judges, Ruth*. Peabody: Hendrickson, 2003.

Harrison, Roland Kenneth. *Introduction to the Old Testament*. Peabody: Prince, 1999.

Heschel, Abraham. *The Prophets*. Peabody: Prince, 2001.

Hubbard, David Allan. *Joel & Amos*. Downers Grove: Inter-Varsity, 1989.

Inch, Morris. *Chaos Paradigm: A Theological Exploration*. Lanham: University Press of America, 1998.

————. *In Christ & On Track*. Lanham: University Press of America, 2008.

————. *Devotions with David*. Lanham: University Press of America, 2000.

————. *Exhortations of Jesus According to Matthew* and *Up From the Depths: Mark as Tragedy*. Lanham: University Press of America , 1997.

————. *The High God*. Kearney: Morris, 2001.

———— and Ronald Youngblood (eds.). *The Living and Active Word of God*. Winona Lake: Eisenbrauns,1983.

————. *Man: The Perennial Question*. Lanham: University Press of America, 1999.

————. "Manifestation of the Holy Spirit," *The Living and Active Word of God* (Inch and Youngblood, eds.), 149-155.

————. *Saga of the Spirit*. Grand Rapids: Baker, 1985.

————. *Service Is As Service Does*. New York: iUniverse, 2006.

————. *Signature of the Spirit*. New York: iUniverse, 2005.

————. *Whispers of Heaven & Heaven According to Matthew*. Fairfax: Xulon, 2002.

Josephus. *The Antiquities of the Jews*.

Keener, Craig. *New Testament*. Downers Grove: InterVarsity, 1993.

Kidner, Derek. *Proverbs*. Downers Grove: Inter-Varsity, 1964.

Knight, George. *Isaiah 56-66*. Grand Rapids: Eerdmans, 1985.

Kuhn, Thomas. *The Structure of Scientific Revolutions*. Chicago: University of Chicago Press, 1966.

Lewis, C. S. *Letter to Giovanni Calabria*.

————. *Miracles*. New York: Macmillan, 1947.

————. *Mere Christianity*. London: Fontana, 1960.

————. *The Screwtape Letters*. London: Fontana, 1955.

Malony, H. Newton (ed.). *Psychology of Religion*. Grand Rapids: Eerdmans, 1991.

Marshall, I. Howard. *Acts*. Downers Grove: Inter-Varsity, 1980.

Mays, James. *Psalms*. Louisville: John Knox, 1994.

Morris, Leon. *1 Corinthians*. Downers Grove: Inter-Varsity, 1990

————. *The Gospel According to John*. Grand Rapids: Eerdmans, 1995.

————. *Luke*. Grand Rapids: Eerdmans, 1990.

Motyer, J. A. "Mystery," *Evangelical Dictionary of the Bible* (Elwell, ed.), 741-742.

Mounce, Robert. *The Book of Revelation*. Grand Rapids: Eerdmans, 1977.

————. *Matthew*. Peabody: Hendrickson, 1991.

Myers, David. "The Mystery of the Ordinary," *Psychology of Religion* (Malony, ed.), 407-412.

Pfeiffer, Charles. *Old Testament History*. Grand Rapids: Baker, 1973.

Schmidt, Alvin. *Under the Influence*. Grand Rapids: Zondervan, 2001.

Schmidt, Wilhelm. *The Origin and Growth of Religion*. London: Matheun, 1935.

Seltzer, Robert. *Jewish People, Jewish Thought*. New York: Macmillan, 1980.

Shaw, George Bernard. *Saint Joan*.

Stauffer, Ethelbert. *Jesus and His Story*. New York: Barbour, 1984.

Stendahl, Krister (ed.). *Immortality and Resurrection*. New York: Macmillan, 1965.

Strobel, Lee. *The Case For Christ*. Grand Rapids: Zondervan, 1998.

Theophilus to Autolycus.

Thielicke, Helmut. *I Believe: The Christian's Creed.* Philadelphia: Fortress, 1968.

Walton, John and Victor Mathews. *Genesis-Deuteronomy.* Downers Grove: Inter-Varsity, 1997.

Wolf, Herbert. *An Introduction to the Old Testament Pentateuch.* Chicago: Moody, 1991.

PART TWO

Baldwin, Joyce, 1972.

Boer, Harry. *A Short History of the Early Church.* Grand Rapids: Eerdmans, 1978.

Boice, James Montgomery. *Acts.* Grand Rapids: Baker, 1997.

Bright, John. *A History of Israel.* Philadelphia: Westminster, 1981.

Clement of Alexandria, *Fragments From the Hypotyposes.*

Cole, R. Alan. *Exodus.* Downers Grover: Inter-Varsity, 1973.

Craddock, Fred. *Luke.* Louisville: John Knox, 1990.

Davids, Peter. *James.* Peabody: Hendrickson, 1993.

Davies, Paul. *God & the New Physics.* New York: Simon & Schuster, 1983.

Duke, Paul. *Irony in the Fourth Gospel.* Atlanta: John Knox, 1985.

Eckstein, Yechiel. *How Firm a Foundation.* Brewster: Paraclete, 1997.

Evans, Craig. *Luke.* Peabody: Hendrickson, 1990.

Farmer, Kathleen. *Proverbs & Ecclesiastes: Who Knows What is Good?* Grand Rapids: Eerdmans, 1996.

Forni, P. M. *Choosing Civility.* New York: St. Martin's Griffin, 2002.

France, R. T. *Matthew.* Grand Rapids: Eerdmans, 1985.

Gadamer, Hans-Georg. *Method and Truth.* New York: Seabury, 1975.

Green, Joel. *The Gospel of Luke.* Grand Rapids: Eerdmans, 1997.

Gundry, Robert. *Matthew.* Grand Rapids: Eerdmans, 1994.

Guthrie, Donald. *New Testament Theology.* Downers Grove: Inter-Varsity, 1981.

Hagner, Donald. *Matthew 11-28.* Dallas: Word, 1995.

Hamlin, E. John. *Judges: At Risk in the Promised Land.* Grand Rapids: Eerdmans, 1990.

Hare, Douglas. *Matthew.* Louisville: John Knox, 1993.

Harrison, Roland Kenneth. *Introduction to the Old Testament.* Peabody: Prince, 1999.

Heschel, Abraham. *The Prophets.* Peabody: Prince, 2001.

Inch, Morris. *Chaos Paradigm: A Theological Exploration.* Lanham: University Press of America, 1998.

———. "Interpreting Luke-Acts," *The Literature and Meaning of Scripture* (Inch and Bullock, eds.), 173-189.

——— and C. Hassell Bullock (eds.). *The Literature and Meaning of Scripture.* Grand Rapids: Baker, 1981.

———. *Scripture As Story.* Lanham: University Press of America, 2000.

———. *Signature of the Spirit.* New York: iUniverse, 2005.

———. *Two Gospel Motifs: The Original Quest & The Messianic Theophany* Lanham: University Press of America, 2001.

———. *Understanding Bible Prophecy.* New York: Harper & Row, 1977.

Irenaeus. *Against Heresies.*

Josephus, *The Antiquities of the Jews.*

Justin Martyr. *Dialogue With Trypho.*

Kidner, Derek. *Genesis.* Downers Grove: Inter-Varsity, 1967.

Marshall, I. Howard. *The Epistles of John*. Grand Rapids: Eerdmans, 1978.
The Martyrdom of Polycarp.
Micklesen, A. Berkeley. *Interpreting the Bible*. Grand Rapids: Eerdmans, 1963.
Mounce, Robert. *The Book of Revelation*. Grand Rapids: Eerdmans, 1977.
———. *Matthew*. Peabody: Hendrickson, 1993.
Origin. *Commentary on John*.
Polkinghorne, John. *Quarks, Chaos & Christianity*. New York: Crossroad, 1997.
Robinson, George. *Essential Judaism*. New York: Pocket, 2000.
Schleiermacher, Friedrich. *Hermeneutics: The Handwritten Manuscripts*. Missoula: Scholars, 1977.
Schmidt, Alvin. *Under the Influence: How Christianity Transformed Civilization*. Grand Rapids: Zondervan, 2001.
Stauffer, Ethelbert. *Jesus and His Story*. New York: Knopf, 1960.
Stendahl, Kreister. *The Bible and the Role of Women*. Philadelphia: Fortress, 1979.
Starrett, T. Norton. *How to Understand Your Bible*. Downers Grove: InterVarsity, 1974.
Tertullian. *The Apology*.
———. *On Prayer*.
.Thiselton, Anthony. *The Two Horizons*. Grand Rapids: Eerdmans, 1980.
Vawter, Bruce and Leslie Hoppe. *Ezekiel: A New Heart*. Grand Rapids: Eerdmans, 1991.
Walton, John and Victor Matthews. *Bible Background Commentary: Genesis-Deuteronomy*. Downers Grove: Inter-Varsity, 1997.
Wenham, Gordon. *Genesis 1-15*. Dallas: Word, 1991.
Williams, David. *Acts*. Peabody: Hendrickson, 1993.
Witherington, Ben III. *The Jesus Quest: The Third Search For the Jew of Nazareth*. Downers Grove: InterVarsity, 1997.
Wolf, Herbert. *An Introduction to the Old Testament Pentateuch*. Chicago: Moody, 1991.

INDEX

ABOUT THE AUTHOR

Morris Inch is Professor Emeritus of Biblical Studies at Wheaton College, Wheaton, Illinois. He has served in other capacities, including President of the Institute of Holy Land Studies (renamed Jerusalem University College), Jerusalem, Israel. Retired for the third time, he continues to add to a list of about forty published books.